D0844672

DattnerArchitects

Introduction

Kent L. Barwick

The old tourist joke, "New York will be a great place if they ever get it finished," seems freshly relevant. Our skyline is dominated by the spires of cranes. The sidewalks are clogged by construction bridges. Street walls are hung with gauzy nettings, soon to be drawn aside like a giant theatrical curtain to reveal a new addition which will immediately alter for better or worse the collective face of the surrounding block. And as these dramatic curtain raisings proceed block by block at an astounding pace, one begins to get a sense of the city we are becoming.

Optimism, energy, and a staggering scent of affluence are in the air. Expensive shops are giddy with visitors from all over the world. Luxury buildings by world-class designers are springing up in what used to be marginal neighborhoods. At night, many of the upper floors are dark, suggesting the new owners are themselves citizens of the world. No one need worry that New York will become like Venice, a place with no local reality, but it's clear that our growing success as a world city can have consequences. As the city's streets become more crowded, more intense, and more international, the value of a civic sphere for local New Yorkers becomes increasingly significant. The quality, the utility, and — dare we say it — the beauty of the public spaces where New Yorkers gather have more impact on our lives than the fleeting glance we are offered of international icons constructed for essentially private use.

New York's record of success in creating outstanding civic buildings and spaces is mixed. Despite venerable early models like C.B.J. Snyder's brilliant series of public schools and Olmsted and Vaux's pioneering parks, too much of what's been built for the public over the years has been dreary. It is cause for celebration, therefore, to see the sustained output of a small firm that has brought verve, good design sense, and persistent ingenuity to an astonishing range of public commissions. Of course, Dattner Architects undertakes all kinds of work (including at present a large office complex for the Federal Government), but what stands out over decades is a genuine commitment to the idea of public architecture and the vigor to address very different kinds of problems with a fresh eye.

As a young parent in the 1960s, I hauled my children to playgrounds far from our own neighborhood that I later learned were designed by Dattner. They were more fun for kids because the structures were both engaging and less defining in terms of limiting the imagination. Like Mumford's description of the city as a stage for man, these little urban places were endlessly adaptable stages for kids who needed hills or castles or forts, or kitchens or clubs or whatever the negotiated consensus game of the moment required. Knowing by accident this early history of Dattner's work on playgrounds made me wonder if the common element of the firm's often award-winning designs for public schools, libraries, recreational centers, subway kiosks, rooftop gardens, boathouses, and even highway toll booths might be some childlike quality of playfulness. After all, the work is clearly joyful (even the sanitation garages and salt storage facilities give pleasure), but of course my theory was exactly backwards. What made the playground work wasn't playfulness but attention to the real needs of people.

There isn't a signature style of the Dattner firm, but there is an embedded signature ambition which stretches from the latest green housing project all the way back 40 years to the playground. It's engagement. It's understanding how people relate to a place, be they kayakers, scholars in the Schomburg Center, or senior citizens stepping carefully into the pool at Asphalt Green.

This ethic — easy to verbalize, hard to live up to — is the secret ingredient in successful civic architecture, and the only way to create a city to which its people feel connected.

Kent L. Barwick is Past President of
the Municipal Art Society of New York

Contents

Culture & Education

Housing

Community & Recreation

Commerce & Industry

Infrastructure

Timeline

1960s–1970s

1

2

3

1990s

10

11

12

13

14

19

20

21

22

23

24

2000s

30

31

32

33

34

35

40

41

42

43

1980s

4

5

6

7

8

9

15

16

17

18

25

26

27

28

29

36

37

38

39

44

45

46

Timeline

1960s–1970s

1964–1972	1976–1980	1978–1993
Estée Lauder Laboratories	Estée Lauder Automated Storage Retrieval Facility	Riverbank State Park
Melville, NY	Melville, NY	New York, NY
1	2	3

1990s

1989–1994	1989–1995	1990–1993	1990–1997	1993–1997
Asphalt Green AquaCenter	Estée Lauder Corporate Headquarters	Clinton Gardens	Leake & Watts Carol & Frank Biondi Education and Athletic Center	Leake and Watts Services, Inc. Cottages
New York, NY	New York, NY	New York, NY	Yonkers, NY	Yonkers, NY
10	11	12	13	14

1995–1998	1995–2000	1996–1998	1997–2000	1997–2002	1997–2003
New York Botanical Garden Discovery Center	Berkeley Carroll School Athletic Center	Estée Lauder Distribution Center	Engine Company 75, Ladder Company 33, Battalion 19	33rd Police Precinct House	LaValle Athletic Stadium
Bronx, NY	Brooklyn, NY	Lachen, Switzerland	Bronx, NY	New York, NY	Stony Brook, NY
19	20	21	22	23	24

2000s

2000–2002	2000–2007	2000–2006	2001	2001–2005	2002
McBurney YMCA	Myrtle–Wyckoff Station Complex	Hudson River Park Segments 6 and 7	205 East 59th St.	Bronx Library Center	Bowling Green Station Canopy
New York, NY	Brooklyn, NY	New York, NY	New York, NY	Bronx, NY	New York, NY
30	31	32	33	34	35

2005	2005	2006	2006
Intrepid Sea, Air and Space Museum Master Plan	Klein Campus Center Dwight Englewood School	Ray and Joan Kroc Community Center	IS/HS 362
New York, NY	Englewood, NJ	Staten Island, NY	Bronx, NY
40	41	42	43

Dattner Architects

1980s

1979–1984
Wien Stadium,
Columbia University
New York, NY

4

1983–1998
Estée Lauder
Research
Laboratories
Melville, NY

5

1984–1988
PS 234
New York, NY

6

1985–1992
Intermediate
School IS 218
New York, NY

7

1988–1997
Prototype Intermediate
Schools Manhattan
Brooklyn, Queens

8

1989–1992
Oakwood Beach
Sludge Treatment
Facility
Staten Island, NY

9

1994–1996
Hertz Orlando Airport Facility
Orlando, FL

15

1994–1998
Goodwill Games Swimming and
Diving Complex
East Meadow, NY

16

1994–2002
Coney Island Lifeguard Stations
Brooklyn, NY

17

1995–1998
New York Athletic Club Pool
New York, NY

18

1997–2001
Administration
for
Children's
Services
New York, NY

25

1997–1999
Primary School 15
Yonkers, NY

26

1998/2002
Con Ed East 16th Street
Service Center
New York, NY

27

1998–2007
Staten Island Jewish Community Center
Staten Island, NY

28

1999–2002
University of Pennsylvania
Pottruck Health &
Fitness Center
Philadelphia, PA

29

2002–2007
Schomburg Center
New York, NY

36

2002
Columbus Circle Station Complex Rehabilitation
New York, NY

37

2003
Marine Transfer Stations
New York, NY

38

2004
Battery Park City Parks
Conservancy
Maintenance Facility
New York, NY

39

2006
Via Verde – The Green
Way (NHNY)
Bronx, NY

44

2008
PS 276
Battery Park City
New York, NY

45

2008
Piers 92 & 94
New York, NY

46

culture
& education

Bronx Library Center

Location: **Bronx, New York**
Client: **The New York Public Library**
Area: **78,000 sf**
Design/Completion: **2002/2005**
Awards: **Citation for Design Excellence AIA New York State, New York City Green Building Award US Environmental Protection Agency, Honorable Mention Environmental Design + Construction Excellence in Design Award, GE Edison Lighting Award of Excellence**

The new Bronx Library Center replaces the former Fordham Branch Library. The facility provides expanded circulation and reference collections, cutting-edge information technology, a full range of education, business and technology training for all ages, literacy classes, and English language proficiency programs. The BLC also houses the Latino and Puerto Rican Cultural Center, with extensive bilingual collections, educational and cultural programs, and multimedia exhibits. The building maximizes collection and seating areas on this tight urban site. Flexible open floor plans and abundant natural light characterize the interior. The project received LEED® Silver Certification from the United States Green Building Council. It is the first public building in New York City to receive LEED® Silver certification.

a.

b.

a. Main stair
b. Section

Opposite page:
Street view

Next page:
View from
E. Kingsbridge Rd.

a.

b.

c.

d.

a. 5th floor reading room
b. Children's floor
   reading area
c. View of exterior
   terrace
d. Children's floor

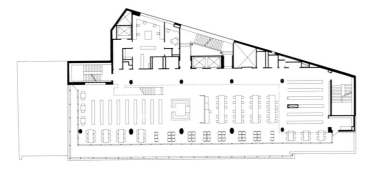

a.

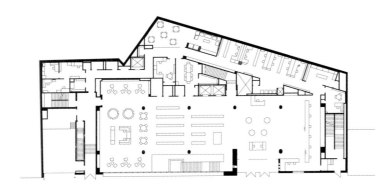

b.

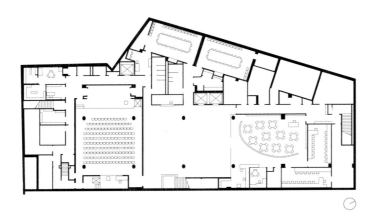

c.

d.

a. 4th floor plan
b. 1st floor plan
c. Concourse plan
d. 4th floor reading room

1 Light shelf
2 Uplight
3 Mechanical shade
4 Perimeter heater
5 Thermally broken curtain wall
6 Low-E glass
7 Sloped soffit

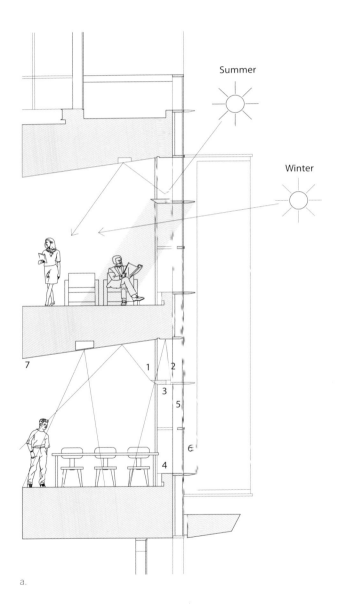

Summer

Winter

a.

b.

c.

d.

a. Exterior wall section
b. East façade
c. View from Fordham Rd.
d. Stair to concourse
   level

Schomburg Center

Location: **Manhattan, New York**
Client: **New York Public Library,**
NYC Department of Design and Construction
Area: **16,000 sf**
Design/Completion: **2002/2007**

The renovation of the Schomburg Center for Research in Black Culture includes the creation of a new Center for Scholars as well as the renovation of several key public spaces. A new glass façade complete with a video wall viewable at night from Malcolm X Boulevard — along with a prominent new entry — announce the library to the neighborhood. A new street-level gallery was created by inserting a partial floor in the former double-height reading room. The reading room can be seen from the gallery and has been reconfigured to reveal a soaring ceiling with acoustic wood panels. The room is the dramatic setting for Aaron Douglas's four signature 1934 murals titled *Aspects of Negro Life*. The new Center for Scholars has a Scholar's Forum for readings and lectures, a conference room, and private offices for the scholars.

The project includes the renovation of the reading/reference areas, electronic research area, Photo Print Vault Room, stacks, and entrance lobby. The building's systems and electronic/computerized control systems were completely upgraded.

a.

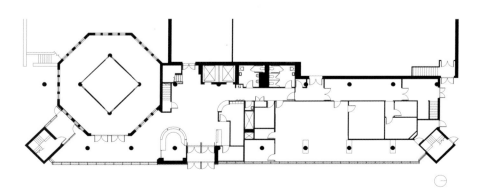

b.

c.

d.

a. Lobby
b. Ground floor plan
c. Video wall
d. Entrance

a.

b.

a. Exhibition gallery
b. Center for Scholars
c. Reading room

c.

Queens West Branch Library

Location: **Queens, New York**
Client: **Queens Borough Public Library**
Area: **22,000 sf**
Design: **2002 study**

Situated within the site of a new high-rise residential development, this branch library will provide a public amenity for the entire neighborhood. The building is situated on New York's East River, opposite the United Nations, offering postcard views of the Manhattan skyline.

The building mediates between urban and landscaped areas, presenting a planted roof — a true "fifth elevation" to the hundreds of residential apartments overlooking the site. The roof is designed to collect storm water runoff and minimize reflected heat, and will require minimal maintenance and irrigation.

The one-story building rises up along Center Boulevard, creating a high street wall. At the south and west sides, deep structural fins frame views towards the river and control sunlight penetration into the reading areas. A glass-screened reading terrace offers views across the river while providing protection from the wind and sun.

Sustainable features include the planted roof, natural daylighting and ventilation, an efficient mechanical plant, as well as recyclable, locally produced building materials.

a.

b.

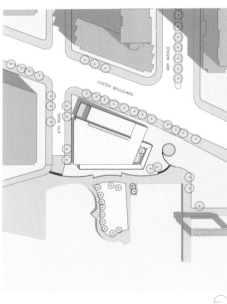

c.

a. Model
b. West elevation
c. Site plan

Jackson Heights Branch Library

Location: **Queens, New York**
Client: **Queens Borough Public Library**
Area: **49,000 sf**
Design: **2003/2008**

The new library, in the Historic Landmark District of Jackson Heights, will replace and greatly expand the original branch library built in the 1950s.

The building accommodates adult and children's reading areas, a 150-seat auditorium, and a variety of class and conference rooms to serve the library and community programs. The five-story structure responds to its context by preserving the scale of the street wall and echoing the rhythmic character and materials of the surrounding apartment buildings. The front façade is conceived as a frame for glass and terra cotta clad panels.

Open to views from the street at the lower levels, the spacing of the solid panels becomes tighter on the higher floors where sun exposure is greater. At the top, the building is set back from the street to form a protected reading terrace located off the children's floor.

The rear elevation is composed of a series of translucent, solid, and transparent panels, combining controlled views into a small garden and privacy for the surrounding neighbors. All enclosed spaces and building services are located along the two side walls — leaving the majority of the floors open for flexible reading and stack areas as well as natural daylight and views.

a.

b.

a. Street level section
b. View from street

Administration for Children's Services

Location Manhattan, New York
Client: NYC Administration for
Children's Services, NYC Department
of Design & Construction
Area: 144,000 sf
Design/Completion: 1997/2001
Awards: Preservation League of New
York State Excellence in Historic
Preservation Award, New York Landmarks
Conservancy Preservation Award, New
York City Art Commission Award for
Excellence in Design

This adaptive reuse of an historic 1907
McKim, Mead & White building creates a
multi-use facility providing a supportive
environment for the intake and overnight
housing of children awaiting foster care
placement. Temporary accommodations
on the second and third floors include
sleeping and dining areas, interview rooms,
classrooms, and indoor and outdoor play
areas serving approximately 110 children.

The three upper floors house the
Satterwhite Training Academy, with
classrooms, computer training rooms, a
distance learning center, and administrative
and staff offices. A 237-seat auditorium and
a conference center are located on the first
floor. The new auditorium was inserted
within the original building courtyard and
a children's outdoor play area was created
above the auditorium.

The ACS Children's Center was the first
major "green" demonstration project for
the New York City Department of Design
and Construction and was profiled by
New York State Energy Research and
Development Authority (NYSERDA)
as an energy efficient building.

a.

b.

c.

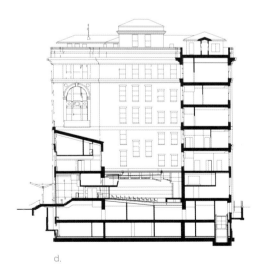

d.

a. Street view
b. Entrance detail
c. Restored Guastavino vaults
d. Section through new auditorium

Queens Vocational & Technical High School

Location: **Queens, New York**
Client: **New York City School Construction Authority**
Owner: **New York City Department of Education**
Area: **194,000 sf total,**
100,000 sf renovation; 94,000 sf addition
Completion: **2005**

Constructed circa 1929 as a continuing education facility, Queens Vocational High School offers academic and vocational curricula in the areas of Cosmetology, Plumbing Technology, and Electric/ Electronic Technologies. The existing facilities were overcrowded and lacked essential elements required for an up-to-date high school program.

The new addition adds science demonstration and technology laboratories, a kitchen/cafeteria suite, a gymnasium suite, library and guidance suite, and administrative support spaces. Selected spaces in the existing building were renovated for new academic program uses and associated mechanical and electrical/ communication systems were upgraded to enable the new addition and existing building to function as an integrated whole. Handicapped accessibility is provided to all floor levels of the existing building and the new addition.

a.

b.

a. Street view
b. Gymnasium

Primary School PS 79 Addition

Location: **Bronx, New York**
Client: **New York City School Construction Authority**
Owner: **New York City Department of Education**
Area: **65,141 sf addition; 8,100 sf renovation**
Design/Completion: **2006/2010**

PS 79 is a five-story turn-of-the-century building located in the University Heights section of the Bronx. The schoolyard directly behind the existing building is the site for the new addition. The expansion, renovation, and reconfiguration of many of the existing spaces provide age appropriate school and playground organization — improving pedestrian and service access and ADA accessibility to the site and building. Community access and use of school facilities is also improved by the new addition. In order to recapture as much of the existing play yard as possible, the roof on the cafeteria has been designed as an outdoor play space serving the entire student body. The project reflects the city's need to adapt school programs to sites with limited area.

a.

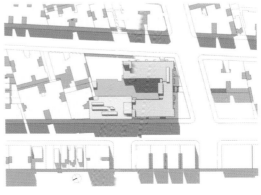

b.

a. Street view
b. Site plan

Primary / Intermediate School
PS 276

Location: **Manhattan, New York**
Client: **New York City School Construction Authority**
Owner: **New York City Department of Education**
Area: **125,000 sf**
Completion: **2010**

As part of New York's sustainable design initiative, this project will be one of the first in the city to be built under the School Construction Authority's Green Schools Guide, developed by Dattner Architects in 2007. An unusual example of a "high-rise" school, the eight-story building's massing and elevations reflect the vertical arrangement of the program required by the limited site area. Public assembly spaces, elementary school grades, and pre-K spaces are accommodated on the lower floors. The Middle School classrooms are at the top of the building. Shared spaces — including the library, art rooms, cafeteria and specialized classrooms — are in the middle of the building on the fifth and sixth floors where they are a short distance away from all students. A 10,000-square-foot outdoor play-roof is located on the third floor.

Occupancy sensors and photo-cell controlled switches located in classrooms and office spaces help reduce the building's energy load and large windows maximize the use of natural daylight. Extra insulation of the building skin, photovoltaic panels and an efficient mechanical plant reduce energy costs by 27 percent below State Energy Code requirements. The rooftop photovoltaic array, visible from the surrounding streets, will provide up to a third of the power required to light the building. The project will use 40 percent less water than traditional schools.

a.

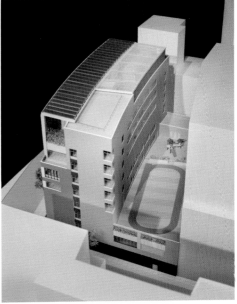

a. Science Terrace
b. Aerial view of play roof
c. View from Battery Park
d. Program diagrams

b.

c.

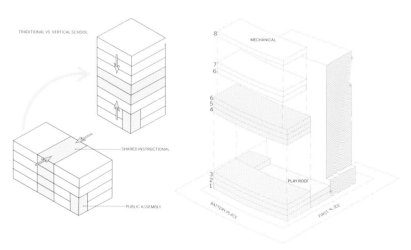

TRADITIONAL VS. VERTICAL SCHOOL

SHARED INSTRUCTIONAL

PUBLIC ASSEMBLY

8 MECHANICAL

7
6

6
5
4

3
2
1 PLAY ROOF

BATTERY PLACE

FIRST PLACE

Shared Program Distribution

Programmatic Stacking Concept

d.

Klein Campus Center, Dwight Englewood School

Location: **Englewood, New Jersey**
Client: **Dwight Englewood School**
Area: **40,000 sf**
Design/Completion: **2003/2005**
Awards: **2007 AIA New Jersey Award of Merit,
New York Construction Magazine Best of 2006
Merit Award**

Located on the landscaped grounds of this private K–12 school, the Klein Campus Center provides a new focal point for the school. The building is integrated into the campus fabric by completing the definition of the central campus quadrangle and linking together two existing buildings. The structure is connected directly to Schenk Hall — which houses the main auditorium and cafeteria. The heart of the project is the 170-seat multipurpose "black box" theater. A skylit atrium over the main stair marks the entrance to this theater. Both the new and existing stage in Schenk Hall share back-of-house theater spaces, transforming the two buildings into one unified performing arts complex. Public circulation spaces are designed to facilitate student interaction and accommodate large groups during events. Facing the interior of the campus, a glazed "interior street" runs the length of the building on both floors — providing circulation, student locker spaces, and study and seating niches overlooking the quadrangle. Classrooms, music rehearsal spaces, administrative spaces, and an expanded cafeteria are located on the more public side of the building, facing the street.

a.

b.

c.

a. Interior street
b. West elevation
c. Campus plan

Next page:
View from bridge

a.

b.

c.

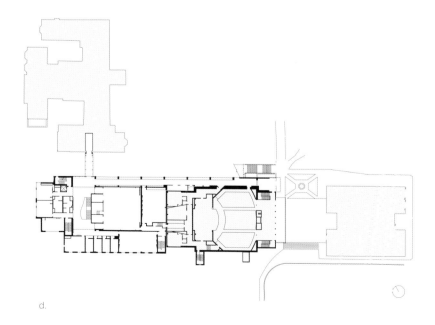

d.

a. Auditorium lobby
b. Campus walk
c. Auditorium
d. 2nd floor plan

The New Settlement Community Campus

Location: Bronx, New York
Client: New York City School Construction Authority, New York City Department of Education, Settlement Housing Fund
Area: 172,500 sf
Design/Completion: 2007/2011
In collaboration with Edelman Sultan Knox Wood Architects

The New Settlement Community Campus offers an innovative model for mixed-use school and community development through a partnership between the New York City Department of Education and the Settlement Housing Fund — a nonprofit housing and social service organization. The new campus comprises two schools serving 1,080 students — Pre-K through High School — as well as a Community Center featuring a swimming pool, multi-purpose rooms and a landscaped roof terrace. The campus is organized in an L-shaped configuration. A commons wing containing the gymnasium, auditorium, and the community center runs along Jerome Avenue, providing a buffer from the adjacent elevated trains. A classroom wing along the side street orients classrooms away from the train noise. The library occupies a honorific place at the corner, cantilevered over and sheltering the main entry. The L-shaped building encloses landscaped outdoor play areas and an amphitheater for school and community gatherings. Contrasting brick colors and patterns, window openings, and stair towers articulate the wings and express the dynamic presence of the campus in this Bronx community.

a.

b.

c.

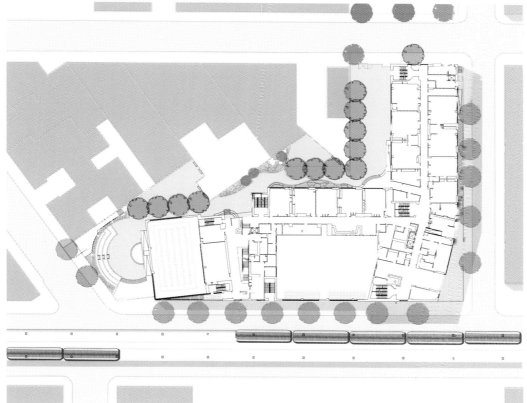

d.

a. Aerial view
b. Façade concept
c. View from Jerome Ave.
d. Ground floor plan

Intermediate School / High School 362 Bronx

Location: Bronx, New York
Client: New York City School
Construction Authority
Owner: New York City Department of Education
Size: 188,700 sf
Design/Completion: 2004/2008

IS/HS 362 combines three independent schools — two high schools and a middle school — with a special education facility in a single building. Each of the three schools accommodates 600 students, while the special education component accommodates 120 students. The building is composed of two main elements, an expansive ground floor covering the entire site, and a multistory, L-shaped classroom wing. Separate gymnasium and auditorium volumes match the scale of the surrounding residential neighborhood. These shared program spaces, as well as the library and cafeteria, are organized around along a skylit interior street, which provides a sense of orientation and an inviting atmosphere at the entry level. Each of the three main schools occupies a single floor, accessed by its own stair and "front door," giving each school unit a more intimate and separate identity within the larger whole.

a.

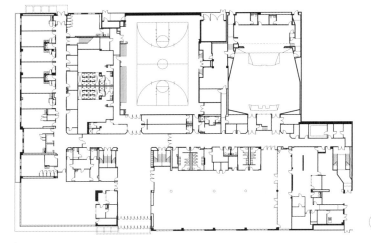

a. Gymnasium exterior
b. Ground floor plan

Opposite page:
Main entrance

b.

a.

b.

c.

d.

a. Auditorium
b. Library
c. Gymnasium
d. Interior street

Westchester Children's Museum

Location: Rye, New York
Area: 40,000 sf
Client: Westchester Children's Museum
Design/Completion: 2006/2009

One of the most beloved icons of Westchester County is the Historic Rye Playland located directly on Long Island Sound. Two Art Deco buildings on the boardwalk at Rye Playland, built circa 1920, have been identified as the site of the future Westchester Children's Museum. These pavilion buildings, comprising the North and South Bathhouses, offer nearly 40,000 square feet for exhibitions, public programs, classrooms, and a performance space — as well as a café, gift shop, gathering areas, and outdoor play structures. These Playland pavilions offer dramatic opportunities to adapt and reuse this beautiful landmark. This remarkable location will enable the Westchester Children's Museum to take advantage of Long Island Sound in its environmental programming, while the architectural character of the buildings creates a unique setting for a children's museum.

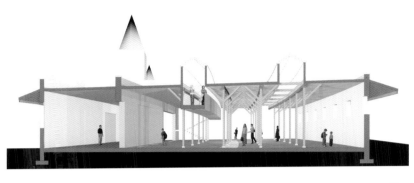

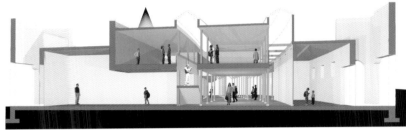

a.

b.

a. Sections
b. Boardwalk view
c. Model
d. Exhibit floor plan

c.

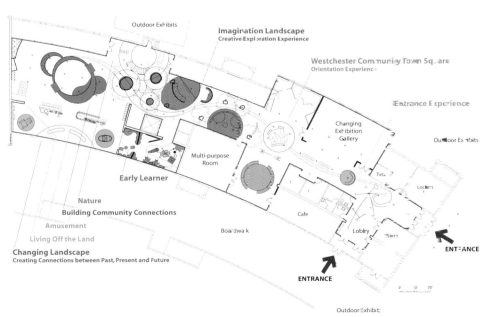

Outdoor Exhibits

Imagination Landscape
Creative Exploration Experience

Westchester Community Town Square
Orientation Experience

Entrance Experience

Changing
Exhibition
Gallery

Outdoor Exhibits

Multi-purpose
Room

Txt.

Lockers

Early Learner

Nature

Building Community Connections

Amusement

Living Off the Land

Cafe

Boardwalk

Lobby

Stairs

Changing Landscape
Creating Connections between Past, Present and Future

ENTRANCE

ENTRANCE

Outdoor Exhibit

d.

47

Han Moory Church

Location: **Englewood, New Jersey**
Client: **Han Moory Church**
Area: **32,000 sf**
Design/Completion: **2007/2009**

The Han Moory Church will occupy a wooded, sloped site in a suburban residential neighborhood. The massing of the building is divided into two parts, reflecting the church's dual role as a spiritual and social center for its Korean congregation. The western volume contains an airy, 300-seat sanctuary. The space is internally focused, without views to the outside. Natural daylight is allowed to filter in through a series of skylights and openings, indirectly brightening the space with a calm, contemplative glow. The eastern volume contains the multipurpose social hall. The entrance lobby, located between these two major spaces, joins the sacred and secular halves of the building. An open skylit stair leads to a lower level housing classrooms, student chapels and a banquet hall. By setting the building into the hillside, the church conforms to zoning height requirements while providing natural light to all occupied spaces. The choice of materials — rough brick, cedar cladding, and zinc roofing — soften the building's geometry, and emphasize its connection to the earth. To preserve the maximum amount of green areas half of the required parking spots are located below the building and accessed by a ramp concealed by the landscape.

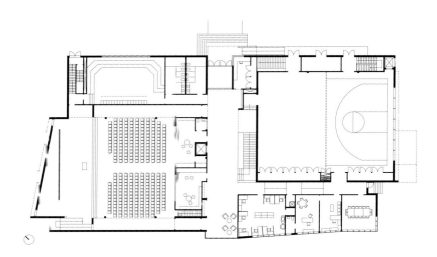

a.

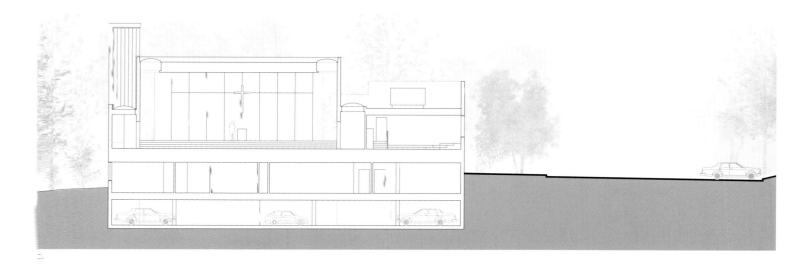

b.

c.

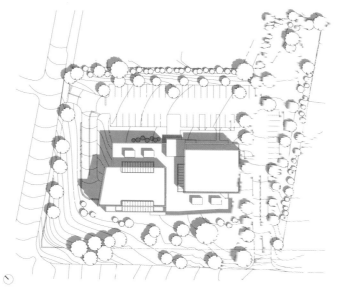

d.

a. Floor plan
b. Section at sanctuary
c. View from southwest
d. Site plan

housing

205 East 59th Street

Location: **Manhattan, New York**
Client: **The Donald Zucker Organization**
Size: **62 Residences, Third Avenue Commercial**
Design/Completion: **2001/2005**
Awards: **Concrete Industry Board Award of Merit**

This 26-story residential tower rises above a commercial base fronting on Third Avenue in mid-town Manhattan. Entered on East 59th Street through a dramatic entrance lobby with stone walls and a waterfall, the slender tower accommodates three apartments per floor. On alternate floors, the apartments feature 22-foot-high living rooms with tall corner windows offering panoramic views of the Manhattan skyline. The building is a poured concrete frame, enclosed with precast concrete panels faced in brick. Delicate perforated steel balcony railings and sun-screens contrast with the vibrant colored precast panels, and the double-height living room windows animate the façade.

a.

a. Street view
b. Entrance

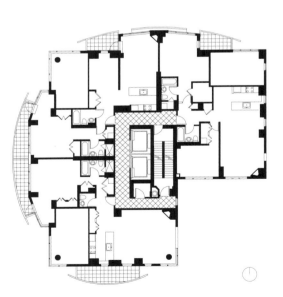

a. Kitchen
b. Plan A
c. Plan B
d. Living room

a.

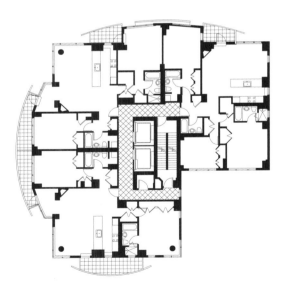

b.

c.

d.

Via Verde – The Green Way

Location: Bronx, New York
Clients: Phipps Houses, Jonathan Rose
Companies, New Housing New York Steering
Committee, AIANY, NYC Department of
Housing Preservation and Development,
NYS Energy Research and
Development Authority
Size: 221 units, 30,000 sf Community
Health Center/Retail
Design/Completion: 2006/2011
PRDG Team: Phipps Houses
Jonathan Rose Companies, Dattner
Architects, Grimshaw Architects

Via Verde – The Green Way is an affordable, sustainable housing complex comprising 222 apartments in three distinct building types — a 21-story tower at the north end of the site, a 6- to 14-story mid-rise duplex building in the middle, and 2- to 4-story townhouses to the south. The project is the result of the New Housing New York Legacy Project, an international architectural competition. The project reflects a public commitment to create the next generation of social housing and seeks to provide a setting for healthy, sustainable living.

A dynamic garden serves as the organizing element and spiritual identity for the community. The garden begins at ground level as a courtyard and then spirals upwards through a series of programmed, south-facing roof gardens, creating a promenade that culminates in a sky terrace with dramatic views to the south. The multifunctional gardens create opportunities for active gardening, fruit and vegetable cultivation, passive recreation, and social gathering, while also providing the benefits of storm water control and enhanced insulation. The buildings take the form of a "tendril," rising from grade to the tower, enclosing the courtyard and emphasizing a relationship to the natural world.

A main point of entry leads to residential lobbies and townhouse entries located around a courtyard. The ground floor features retail, community facility spaces, and live-work units, creating a lively street presence. Above the main entrance overlooking the street and courtyard are resident community spaces — including a fitness center and homework center. The top floor of the tower contains a multi-purpose community room with access to terraces and spectacular views.

Via Verde – The Green Way will set new standards for the sustainable design of affordable housing. The complex is being designed to achieve a LEED® NC Gold Certification.

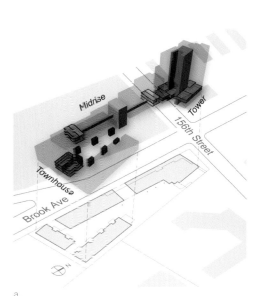

a.

b.

c.

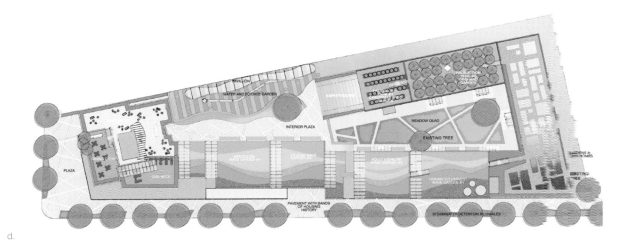

d.

a. Massing diagram
b. Entrance
c. View from tower
d. Site plan

Next page:
View from Brook Ave.

a

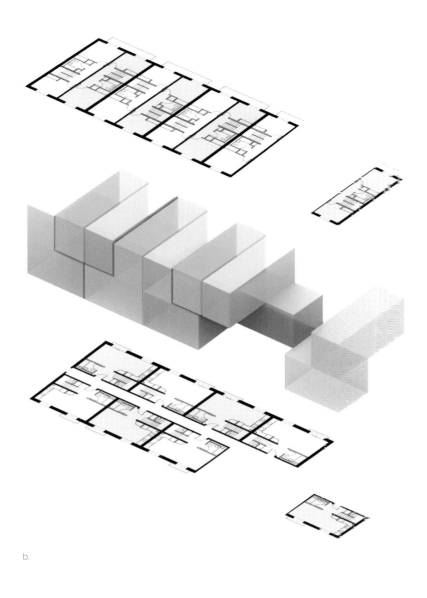

b.

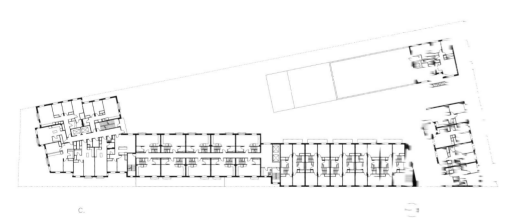

c.

a. Roof gardens
b. Mid-rise duplex units
c. Level 4 Plan

David and Joyce Dinkins Gardens

Location: **Manhattan, New York**
Client: **Jonathan Rose Companies / Harlem Congregations for Community Improvement**
Size: **85 units**
Design/Completion: **2004/2008**

David and Joyce Dinkins Gardens is an affordable housing development located in Harlem, comprising 85 apartments — ranging from studio to two bedroom units — to house low-income families and youths aging out of foster care.

The building includes a community center with classroom and activity spaces. A landscaped garden area provides an outdoor recreational space for residents and re-establishes a community garden formerly located on the site. The brick building is organized into bays in contrasting brick colors to provide scale and visual interest. Brick banding and a rusticated base emphasize the residential character of the building. Two recessed window wall bays interrupt the brick façade to mark the residence and community center

entries and open the façade to the community. The project is participating in the Enterprise Green Communities Initiative, which promotes sustainable design for affordable housing. Sustainable design features include: use of EnergyStar appliances and light fixtures; low-flow plumbing fixtures; use of "green" and recycled materials; enhancement of indoor air quality through insulation and optimized, unit-by-unit ventilation; native, low-maintenance planting; and resident education. A green roof is installed on the sixth floor setback roof and a roof terrace shaded by a trellis for use by the residents is located at this level. A rainwater harvesting system provides water for irrigation of the garden, and sunshades are used for solar control at south facing windows.

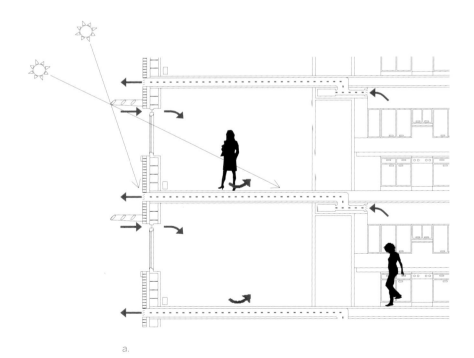

a.

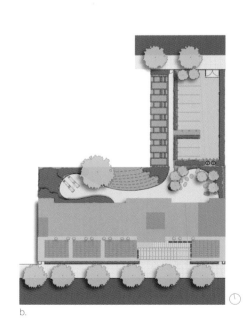

b.

c.

a. Wall section
b. Site plan
c. Street view

Myrtle Avenue Development

Location: **Brooklyn, New York**
Client : **Red Apple Group**
Size: **765 units**
Design/Completion: **2006/2011**

The Myrtle Avenue Development is located in downtown Brooklyn along Myrtle Avenue near its intersection with Flatbush Avenue. The development comprises 765 apartments, including 325 market-rate apartments in a 38-story tower and 440 mixed-income apartments in mid-rise buildings ranging from 8 to 14 stories in height. Under a "50-30-20" mixed income housing plan, there is a significant component of affordable housing. The development includes approximately 150,000 square feet of commercial space and sub-grade parking. The dramatic

apartment tower rises to 400 feet — offering spectacular panoramic views. The adjoining mid-rise buildings step down from 14 stories to 8 stories to the east, mediating in scale between the height and density of downtown Brooklyn and the lower scale neighborhood of Fort Greene to the east. A brick base along Myrtle Avenue balances the residential character of the neighborhood with a continuous retail presence along the street. The buildings have a contemporary aesthetic that expresses the resurgence of Downtown Brooklyn.

a.

b.

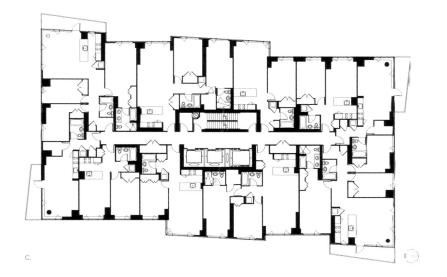

c.

a. Aerial view
b. View at Myrtle Ave.
c. Tower plan

50 Howard Street

Location: **Manhattan, New York**
Client: **Roag Inc. & Two Chestnuts Inc.**
Area: **25,000 sf**
Design/Completion: **2005/2009**

50 Howard Street was originally built in 1863 as the New York Soldiers' Depot, where soldiers returning from the Civil War were received and cared for free of charge. The five-story, 25,000 sf structure located in SoHo's Cast Iron Landmark District is being converted into luxury apartments, including one- to four-bedroom apartments. The façade is being fully restored after decades of neglect. The original heavy timber interior structure will be preserved and partially exposed in the new living spaces. A penthouse with a large south facing terrace is being added to the structure, creating a 5,000-square-foot duplex at the top of the building. The ground floor and basement are being converted to retail space, requiring a zoning variance and approval from the Landmarks Preservation Commission.

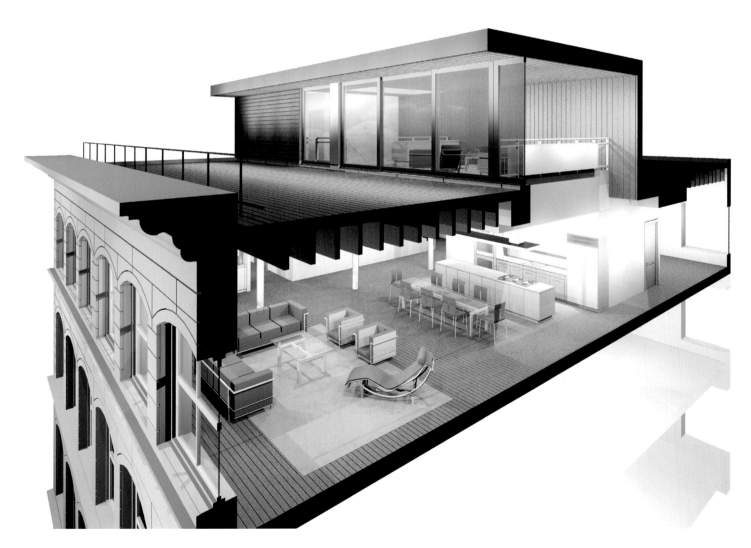

a.

b.

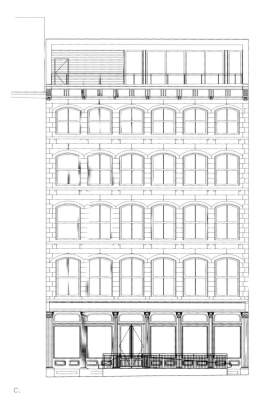

c.

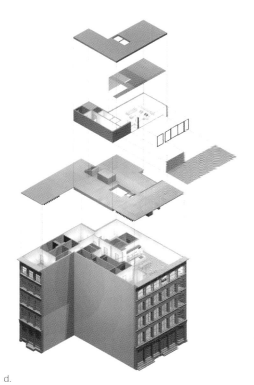

d.

a. Penthouse section
b. Interior
c. Howard St. façade
d. Axonometric

Coney Island Commons

Location: **Brooklyn, New York**
Client: **Coney Island Commons LLC,
NYC Economic Development Corporation,
NYC Department of Housing
Preservation and Development**
Size: **188 units, 40,000 sf Community Center**
Design/Completion: **2007/2011**

Coney Island Commons is an affordable housing complex which will include a community center to be operated by the YMCA of Greater New York. The residential component of the project will contain 152 cooperative units, affordable for low- and middle-income families. The YMCA will provide residents with much-needed recreational and community facilities. The site is within the boundaries of the Coney Island Urban Renewal Area, and is located a block from Coney Island's famous boardwalk and beach. The residential component of the development consists of two buildings of seven and eleven stories that include an assortment of studios, one-, two- and three-bedroom units. The residential component will include a landscaped courtyard on the roof of the YMCA and over a parking area. The community center will include an aquatic center with a lap pool and family recreational pool, a full court gymnasium, fitness and multi-purpose rooms, social rooms, and office spaces. The development features sustainable design elements to conserve resources and promote healthy living for residents and community — including energy efficient mechanical systems, water conserving fixtures, extensive use of natural light and lighting controls, and use of recycled, regionally manufactured and renewable materials. Portions of the community center will feature "green" roofs planted with natural grasses and wildflowers native to a beach environment. The community center and housing project are the latest components of the Coney Island Strategic Plan, which calls for the enhancement of amusements and seaside attractions, establishment of a year-round entertainment destination, and creation of economic opportunities for local residents.

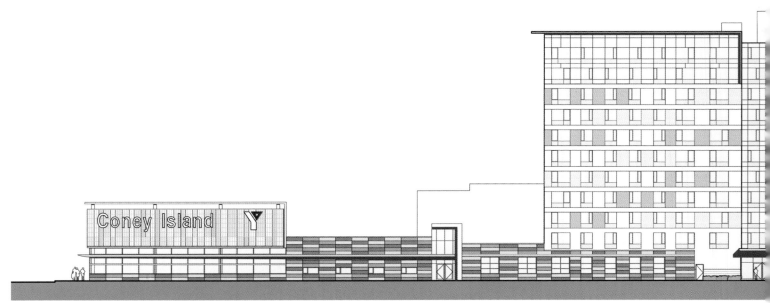

a.

b.

a. Elevation
b Street view
c Ground floor plan
d Site plan

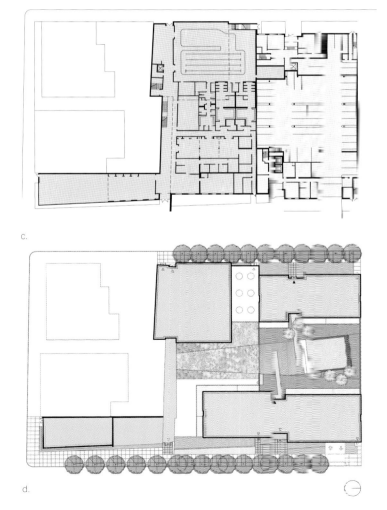

c.

d.

Courtlandt Corners

Location: **Bronx, New York**
Client: **The Phipps Houses Group**
Size: **326 units**
Area: **30,000 sf retail space**
Design/Completion: **2006/2011**

This new affordable housing development is sponsored by The Phipps Houses Group, a nonprofit housing developer, owner, and manager. The sites — Courtlandt Corners I and II — are located on two blocks of the Melrose Commons Urban Renewal Area in the South Bronx and front East 161st Street, the neighborhood's main thoroughfare. A contextual design provides an eight-story building with a retail base. Ten-story sections at the corners provide a gateway to the neighborhood. A seven-story building fronts East 162nd Street. Based on the NYC residential prototype of perimeter buildings with internal green spaces, the buildings are organized around interior landscaped courtyards — on grade at CCI and on the roof of an enclosed parking area at CCII. Brick colors, patterns, and metal panels emphasize a welcoming residential character articulated with a contemporary architectural expression. Apartments range from studios to three-bedroom units, with predominately two-bedroom apartments. The apartments have generous layouts and large windows to provide abundant natural light.

The project is participating in the NYSERDA Multi-Family Performance Program and incorporates sustainable design features, including brownfield redevelopment, stormwater management, low-flow plumbing fixtures, a high-performing building envelope, energy-efficient HVAC systems, EnergyStar appliances and lighting, and attention to indoor environmental quality.

b.

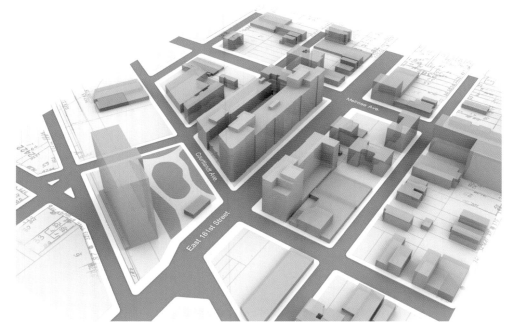

a.

a. Massing study
b. View at E. 161st St.

community
& recreation

Hudson River Park Segments 6 & 7

Location: **Manhattan, New York**
Client: **Hudson River Park Trust**
Area: **2 miles of Waterfront**
Design/Completion: **2000/2007**
Awards: **2006 Award of Merit AIA New York State, New York Construction Magazine 2005 Best of New Construction Award, 2006 Waterfront Conference Featured Project**
In association with MKW + Associates LLC Landscape Architects

The greening of New York City's Hudson River waterfront — historically the site of maritime infrastructure and heavy industry — returns river access to the public. The design of this 2-mile segment of the Hudson River Park along Manhattan's west side transforms the former industrial waterfront into a public amenity, revives boating, and encourages other maritime activities. Three "upland" buildings house classrooms, concessions, restaurants, maintenance spaces, and public restrooms, and three boathouses are distributed along the length of the park between West 26th and West 59th Streets. Based on contrasting prototypes of masonry "upland", or zinc-clad "pier" structures, they are adapted to each particular site or program.

Boathouses at Pier 96, Pier 84, and Pier 66 serve educational and recreational programs. These structures are based on a common prototype adapted to the requirements of their particular site or program. The structures emphasize the principles of environmentally conscious, energy-efficient design, taking advantage of solar orientation, natural daylight, and ventilation. Large sliding doors provide cross ventilation, the interiors receive abundant clerestory lighting, and ridge vents provide natural convection. The Pier 84 service building houses a café, park offices, and public facilities. Sustainable design features include: restoration and protection of habitat; native and drought-resistant plantings; water use reduction and targeted irrigation; maximization of open space; green roof; maximized daylight; site lighting minimizing light pollution; increased natural ventilation; maximized views from buildings; recycled and regional materials; forest council certified woods; benign, non-off-gassing materials; 50-year life cycle; public transportation access; and bicycle storage.

a.

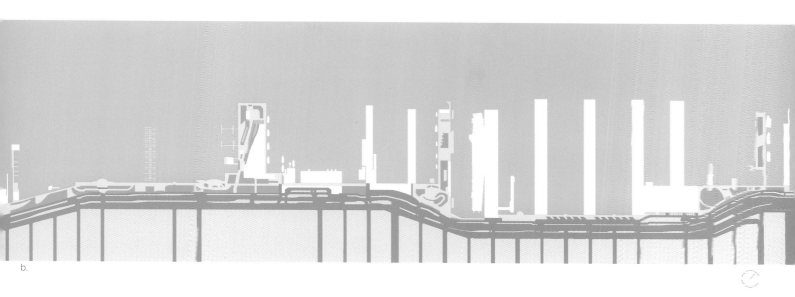

b.

c.

d.

a. Pier 96 Boathouse
b. Site plan of Segments 6 & 7
c. Pier 96
d. Pier 63 water wheel

a.

b.

c.

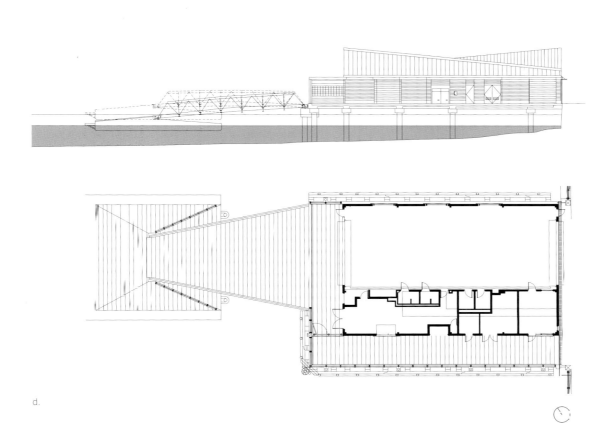

d.

e.

a.

b.

c.

d.

e.

Intrepid Sea, Air and Space Museum Master Plan

Location: **Manhattan, New York**
Client: **Intrepid Sea, Air and Space Museum**
Design/Completion: **2005/2008**

One of New York City's most visited attractions, the Intrepid Museum aims to "honor our heroes, educate the public, and inspire our young people." The USS Intrepid (CV11) aircraft carrier was commissioned in 1943 for service in World War II, served during the Vietnam conflict, and went on to serve as a primary recovery vessel for NASA. The museum features the historic ship, as well as a range of interactive exhibits honoring the events and sailors which made Intrepid a symbol of heroism, dedication, and service. The master plan for the Intrepid will guide the Museum's development and improvement in the short and long term. Previously inaccessible areas like the fo'c'sle and the chain room have been opened to the public. The stair and elevator towers designed for the adjoining Pier 86 improve access to the ship, transform the Intrepid Museum for next generations, and strengthen its connections to the Hudson River Park.

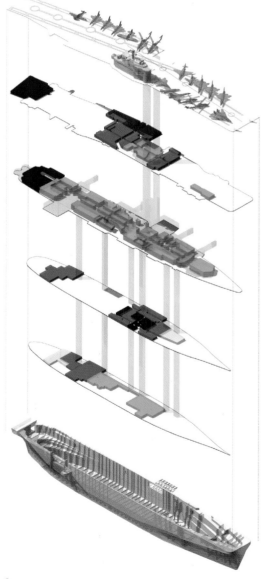

a.

b.

c.

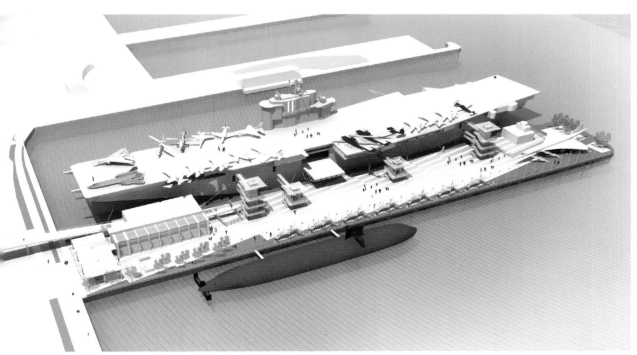

d.

a. Program diagram
b. Access tower
c. Pier 86
d. Aerial view

Kenneth P. LaValle Stadium,
State University of New York at Stony Brook

Location: **Stony Brook, New York**
Client: **State University Construction Fund**
Area: **7,500 spectator seats**
25,887 sf South Building
17,176 sf East Building
Design/Completion: **1997/2003**
Awards: **Concrete Industry Board Award of Merit Pre-Cast, Concrete Industry Board Award of Excellence**

This new 7,500-seat stadium provides an athletic and cultural venue for the State University of New York at Stony Brook in Long Island. Located near the center of this large campus, the stadium accommodates Division I football, soccer, lacrosse, and field hockey. Concerts, graduation, and other cultural activities are also staged in the stadium.

The artificial turf field and adjacent seating are set into the existing grade and surrounded by native-planted berms, giving the stadium a "green" character and reducing its visual impact on the campus and surrounding community. A raised concrete seating structure to the east forms a concourse sheltering a public way open to students during non-game times. The adjacent east building houses press boxes, a VIP observation level, and concession facilities. Sports facilities, lockers, concessions, and additional public facilities are located under the south stands. Future expansion to a capacity of 15,000 is planned.

a.

b.

a. View from field
b. View under stands
c. Cross section

Opposite page:
View from
end-zone seating

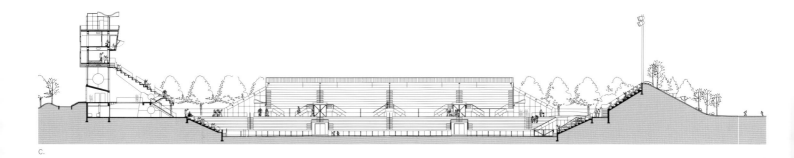

c.

Dattner Architects   Community & Recreation

Ray and Joan Kroc Corps Center

Location: **Staten Island, New York**
Client: **The Salvation Army**
Area: **110,000 sf**
Design/Completion: **2006/2010**

The Ray and Joan Kroc Corps Center is located in the Stapleton community on the north shore of Staten Island. A cantilevered chapel sheathed in zinc is a dramatic form facing the New York Harbor and identifying this center as a Salvation Army facility. The sloping site allows for a three-story building, with the main entrance on the middle floor. The plan is organized around two circulation axes. Visitors enter on a "Sacred Way" connecting the chapel, the worship/performing arts center, and the sacred space on the upper floor. An intersecting central corridor, or "Main Street", organizes the recreation and education program elements. Recreational areas requiring membership are located on the lower level, while unpaid program elements are located on the entry and upper levels. The natatorium is a tall, dramatic space with southern and eastern exposure.

From the street, the three-story glass volume will act as a beacon. n addition to the traditional lap pool, the natatorium will have special pools for family water play, beginner swimmers, and the elderly. A leisure pool with zero-depth entry, a "lazy river" with a gentle current, a therapy pool, and a whirlpool complete this water park. The gymnasium accommodates 200 spectators around a high-school sized basketball court. Fitness and aerobics are located on the lower level, near the locker rooms, and also have views of the harbor.

a.

b.

c.

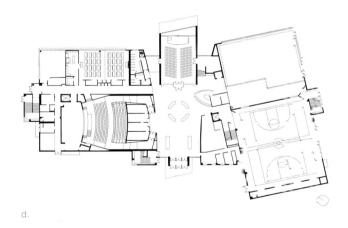

d.

a. Entrance
b. View of natatorium
c. Chapel
d. Entrance level floor plan

YMCA of Greater New York

Locations: **Manhattan and Brooklyn, New York**
Client: **YMCA of Greater New York**
Area: **McBurney YMCA, Manhattan 40,000 sf,**
Harlem YMCA, Manhattan 10,000 sf,
Dodge YMCA, Brooklyn 38,000 sf
Design/Completion: **2000–2003/2002–2005**
Awards: **Building Brooklyn Award of Merit**

Three of the YMCA facilities for the YMCA of Greater New York designed by Dattner Architects are illustrated.

The McBurney YMCA, located in the basement and ground floor levels of a new residential building on West 14th Street, was the first new YMCA to be built in Manhattan in over 75 years. It accommodates a competition 25-yard swimming pool, a gymnasium with handball, volleyball, and basketball courts, two aerobics studios, weight training and large cardiovascular area, locker rooms, and a member's lounge with a view of the natatorium.

The Dodge YMCA, also located in a new residential building, serves the downtown Brooklyn community. Users enter into a soaring double-height atrium. Clear glass walls separate spaces to allow natural light into the interior and provide a sense of openness. The facility includes a full-size gymnasium, daycare facilities, aerobic studios, weight training facilities, community spaces, and a 6-lane, 25-yard swimming pool.

The 1932 Harlem YMCA is a New York City Landmark. The recent renovation reconfigured the lobbies and modernized the natatorium — dramatically transforming it with new lighting, extensive new finishes, restoration of historic elements, and new and upgraded HVAC systems.

a.

b.

c.

d.

a. Dodge YMCA, Lobby
b. McBurney YMCA, Gym
c. Harlem YMCA
   Swimming pool
d. McBurney YMCA
   Lounge

Jewish Community Center of Staten Island

Location: **Staten Island, New York**
Client: **Jewish Community Center
of Staten Island**
Area: **110,000 sf**
Design/Completion: **1998/2006**
Awards: **QBBA Building Award**

The site for the Jewish Community Center of Staten Island lies in an historic district — designed on a predefined footprint within a pre-approved building volume. The new building replaces several outdated facilities and serves a diverse, growing population. The JCC accommodates an indoor and outdoor swimming pool, two gymnasia, an early childhood center, a social hall, fitness center, and a café and lounge. A curved entry wall of Jerusalem stone welcomes members and visitors. A series of themed interior walls organize the building to express the character and culture of the JCC. These walls define major public spaces and express the themes of Remembrance, Life, Learning, and Community. In the skylit lobby, café, and lounges, members can meet and socialize. A skylit stair in the heart of the building connects the three levels of the JCC.

a.

b.

c.

d.

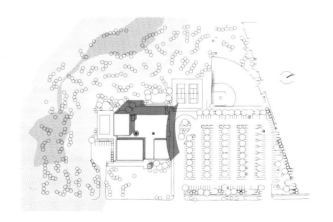

e.

a. Entry detail
b. Lobby
c. Lounge
d. Entrance view
e. Site plan

Pier 40 – The People's Pier

Location: **Manhattan, New York**
Client: **Camp Group LLC,**
Urban Dove, Hudson River Park Trust
Area: **1,400,000 sf**
Proposal: **2007–2008**

The redevelopment of Pier 40 offers an opportunity to create a landmark public space that will be the center of community recreation for decades to come. The People's Pier will be a place where people of all ages can gain access to New York's waterways, build stronger bodies and minds, and enjoy fun and social activity. The plan for Pier 40 calls for the development of a vibrant, community-focused complex bringing together cultural, recreational, and educational uses in a publicly accessible setting. The Pier 40 structure will contain indoor and outdoor athletic facilities, a new high school and college facility, a marina, administrative offices, and community parking. The staging and phasing of the plan allows uninterrupted access to the pier during its redevelopment, keeping the tremendously popular recreational space and parking currently housed at the pier available to the community.

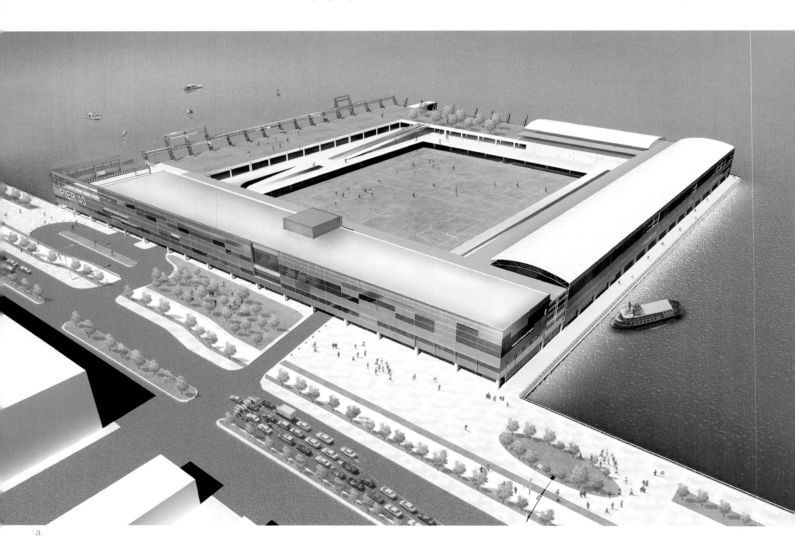

a.

a. Aerial view
b. Roof top lawn
c. View from West St.

b.

c.

Pottruck Health & Fitness Center, University of Pennsylvania

Location: **Philadelphia, Pennsylvania**
Client: **University of Pennsylvania**
Area: **120,000 sf total,**
70,000 sf new,
50,000 sf renovated
Design/Completion: **1999/2002**
Awards: **Buildings Magazine**
New Construction Award of Excellence

The Pottruck Health & Fitness Center joins the existing Gimbel Gym and Sheerr Pool to complete a comprehensive recreation and wellness complex for the University of Pennsylvania. Since its opening, Pottruck has become one of the main campus centers of activity and socialization.

The new wing is a series of largely open "trays" supporting areas for weight training, exercise, yoga, dance, aerobics, and other fitness activities. The existing pool and gymnasium area are rehabilitated, with new locker rooms on the basement level to support both new and renovated facilities.

An interior "street," a campus walk within a skylit atrium, links both buildings. All the activities are visible from this atrium, with a cascading stair providing access to the fitness floors and a bridge to the upper-level gymnasium. The fitness levels step back from the atrium successively on each floor, and cantilever over the exterior campus walk, in order to allow the maximum daylight to reach both interior and exterior streets. Open balconies at the upper levels overlook a climbing wall suspended from the former exterior wall of Gimbel Gym.

a.

a. Interior Street
b. Walnut St. view
c. Exercise studios
d. Section

b.

c.

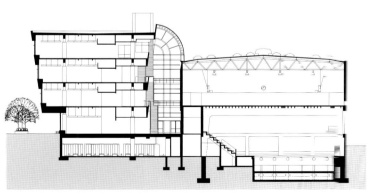

d.

Tennis Pavilion, Princeton University

Location: **Princeton, New Jersey**
Client: **Princeton University**
Area: **7,500 sf**
Design/Completion: **2007/2009**

The new Princeton Tennis Pavilion realizes Princeton's master plan for the Lenz Tennis Center. The two-level facility occupies a pivotal location bridging the levels of the eight varsity competition courts. Tennis coach offices and a glazed meeting room occupy the upper level and are surrounded by a large observation deck with views of all the courts. The lower level encloses locker rooms, toilets, and mechanical and storage space. A large covered deck area on this level provides a gathering area for visiting teams and spectators.

The simple, elegant structure is characterized by slender steel columns, laminated wood beams, wood decking, and steel cable railings. The dramatic zinc-clad roof folds down to become a wall enclosing the upper deck and program spaces.

a.

b.

c.

a. View from campus walk
b. Players' lounge
c. View from courts

commerce
& industry

Nyack Riverspace Master Plan

Location: **Nyack, New York**
Client: **Riverspace Arts**
Area: **250,000 sf**
100,000 sf retail,
100,000 sf residential,
40,000 sf performing arts
Design/Completion: **2008/2012**

The Village of Nyack is a historic river town located on the Hudson, 25 miles from New York City. This downtown revitalization project, located at the center of the village, is intended to reverse a pattern of urban decline brought about by economic stagnation and piecemeal demolition dating back to the 1960s. The 3-acre site currently serves as a municipal parking lot and includes two commercial buildings — one of which houses a 500-seat community theater.

The proposal, consisting of three- to four-story buildings, is a mixed-use development combining cultural, commercial, residential, and retail occupancies. The site has been subdivided into short, pedestrian-friendly blocks by the continuation of existing city streets. The smaller parcels also increase the amount of retail frontage and street parking. A pedestrian path crosses the site, reconnecting a public housing project — previously isolated by the parking lot — to Main Street. A new public plaza has been created at the northeast corner of the site serving as a symbolic link between the old and new parts of downtown. It provides a flexible, generous area for café seating and special events. A new theater building, subsidized by this development, faces the plaza to create an impressive civic presence. Parking for 550 cars is provided in multistory parking behind the theater and in an underground garage below the site.

a.

b.

c.

d.

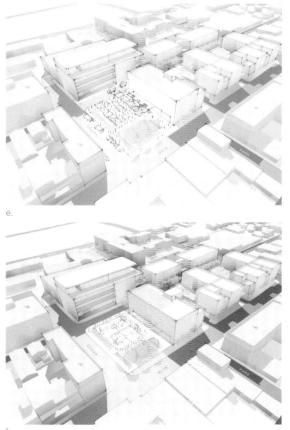

e.

f.

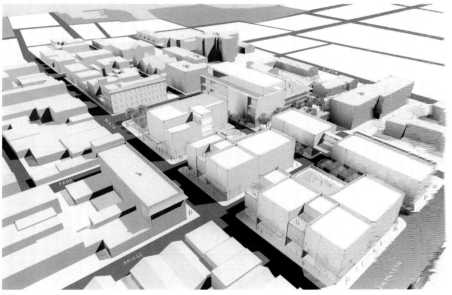

g.

a. Pedestrian walkway
b. Main St
c. Site plan
d. Public plaza
e. Plaza programming
   Farmers' Market
f. Plaza programming
   Basketball tournament
g. Aerial view

Con Edison East 16th Street Service Center

Location: **Manhattan, New York**
Client: **Consolidated Edison Company of New York, Inc.**
Area: **98,000 sf**
Design/Completion: **1998/2002**

Designed to demonstrate contemporary strategies for energy conservation and sustainability, the building houses technicians and equipment for servicing Con Edison's steam, gas, and electric distribution systems throughout Manhattan. The three-story building contains a storage facility for tools, parts, and other materials required for routine and emergency repairs on the ground floor. The second floor houses the various operating departments with muster rooms and locker facilities. The third floor is a flexible, open office floor for engineering and technical support staff, organized around a central core. The sophisticated curtain wall follows the curve of the adjacent FDR drive and offers sweeping views of the East River, maximizing daylight while limiting direct sunlight into the facility. A large skylight brings additional daylight deep into the building.

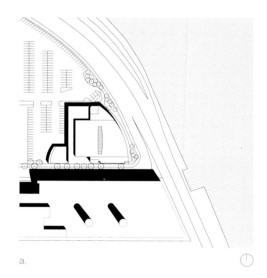

a.

b.

c.

d.

a. Site plan
b. Façade detail
c. View from FDR Dr.
d. View from North
   with Con Edison
   power plant beyond

World Trade Center Proposal

Location: **Manhattan, New York**
Design: **2001**

This proposal for the rebuilding of the World Trade Center sought to honor the victims and the heroism of their rescuers, memorialize the tragedy, communicate our steadfastness to the nation and the world, respect the past — yet turn toward a changed future — incorporating current life-safety, sustainability, and structural knowledge. The proposed 75-story towers turn toward each other as they rise, facing each other directly at their tops. The towers are linked at three transfer floors by bridges allowing access and egress between towers. The original building footprints are preserved for memorial sites. As an iron bar is forged by great heat into a stronger form, the transformation of the towers in itself memorializes the events of 9/11.

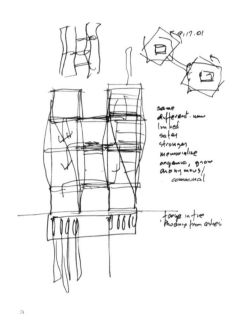

a.

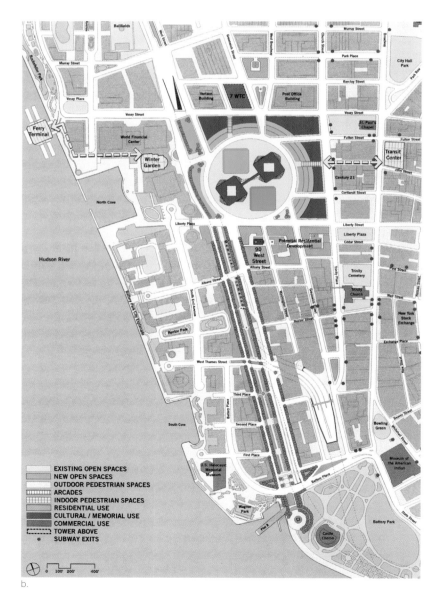

EXISTING OPEN SPACES
NEW OPEN SPACES
OUTDOOR PEDESTRIAN SPACES
ARCADES
INDOOR PEDESTRIAN SPACES
RESIDENTIAL USE
CULTURAL / MEMORIAL USE
COMMERCIAL USE
TOWER ABOVE
SUBWAY EXITS

b.

c.

a. Concept sketch 9.17.2001
b. Site plan
c. View north to linked towers

Steiner Studios

Location: **Brooklyn, New York**
Client: **Steiner Equities Group**
Area: **15 acres**
Design/Completion: **2002/2005**
Studio Interiors by the Janson Design Group

The Steiner Studio complex of buildings, streets, and lots represents a renaissance for the Brooklyn Navy Yard. Where 75,000 people once labored in defense of our country, a 21st-century workplace provides state-of-the-art facilities for the production of a full range of entertainment and information media. Steiner Studios is a self-contained urban precinct within the Navy Yard organized around a central street defined by steel-truss entrance gates. Visitors, actors, production personnel, and stage hands inhabit a new neighborhood offering all the components required to support production: studios, shops, material sales, commissary, post-production, and administrative space.

The studio buildings are true "New Yorkers" — tough on the outside, intelligent and sensitive on the inside. Exteriors are constructed from precast concrete panels with aluminum and glass curtain walls. Concrete walls between sound stages control sound transmission between productions. Studio grid heights of 35 and 45 feet allow for the most demanding set requirements. Ancillary spaces are clustered around the studio spaces to increase production efficiency.

a.

a. Abigail Kirsch Ballroom

Opposite page:
Gateway to complex

424 West 33rd Street

Location: **Manhattan, New York**
Client: **Vectra Management Group**
Area: **162,150 sf existing commercial,
48,000 sf new construction commercial,
51,850 sf new construction residential,
262,000 sf Total Building Area**
Design/Completion: **2008/2011**

The Vectra Management Group commissioned a mixed-use addition to the top of their existing 1913 commercial building. The new addition incorporates six stories of new commercial floors and nine new residential floors. The size of the addition is limited by the NYC Zoning Resolution Hudson Yards Special District and the existing structure will require structural reinforcement. The addition will be clad in a high-performance glass curtain wall and metal panel system,

introduce new high speed elevators to service the tenants, and "float" over the existing masonry building — allowing the existing mechanical systems on the existing roof to remain.

Wind and seismic structural considerations are expressed in the cross-bracing on the south elevation above the existing building. Horizontal trusses support the steel frame for the commercial and residential expansion.

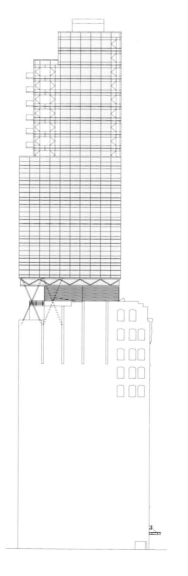

a.

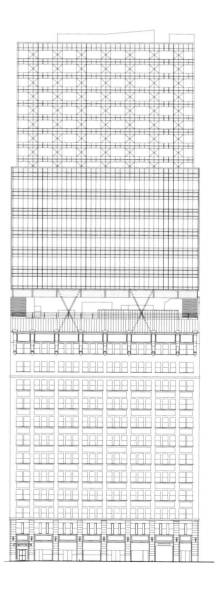

a. Elevations
b. Exterior

Piers 92 / 94
Merchandise Mart

Location: **Manhattan, New York**
Client: **Vornado Realty Trust, Merchandise Mart Properties Inc., NYC Economic Development Corporation**
Area: **425,000 sf**
Design/Completion: **2006/2010**
In association with SMWM Architects

This reinvention and reinvigoration of Piers 92 / 94 brings New York City much-needed tradeshow space and Hudson River Park highly desired public amenities. The project creates 425,000 square feet of exhibition-ready, state-of-the-art waterfront trade show space. The design pairs an inwardly focused trade show facility with a pavilion — an all-weather, glass-enclosed public/private space facing both Midtown Manhattan and the Hudson River. The pavilion can be opened to the outdoors into the adjacent Clinton Cove Park.

New public access will be provided along the northern and western aprons of Pier 94, with a generous open space at the end of the 770-foot-long pier — offering views of the Hudson River, the George Washington Bridge, and New Jersey. The design allows for the integration of a future bridge over Route 9A, connecting DeWitt Clinton Park and Clinton Cove Park by a weather-protected pedestrian access.

a.

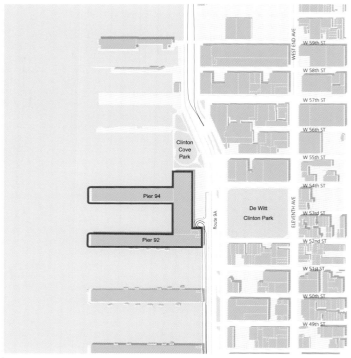

b.

c.

a. Aerial view
b. Site plan
c. View from the water

11

a.

b.

c.

a. Entrance plaza
b. View from southwest
c. Pavilion at Clinton Cove

Battery Park City Parks Conservancy

Location: **Manhattan, New York**
Client: **Battery Park City Parks Conservancy**
Area: **40,500 sf**
Design/Completion: **2007/2009**
Awards: **New York City Green Building Award**
US Environmental Protection Agency

BPC Parks Conservancy's new facility will centralize their extensive maintenance activities and will include vehicle storage, workshop spaces, composting areas, and offices. The facility is located on the lower levels of a high-rise residential building and is being designed to achieve a LEED® Platinum rating under the Corporate Interiors Program. This state-of-the-art space has a four-story atrium bringing natural light into all the spaces. A double-glazed exterior walkway will help cool the space in the summer and heat the space in the winter by controlling air circulation patterns. Treated waste water from the adjacent residential project will be used for washing maintenance vehicles.

a.

a. Section perspective
b. Plan
c. View from south
d. Energy diagrams

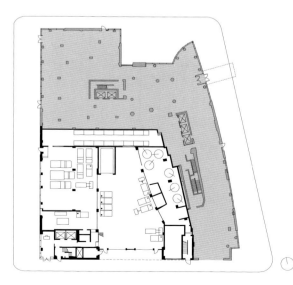

b.

image courtesy Pelli Clarke Pelli Architects

c.

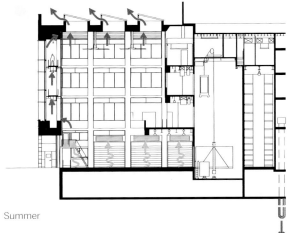

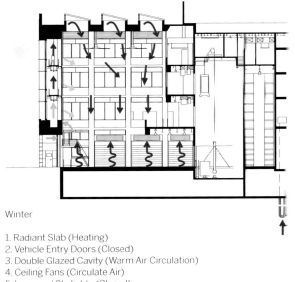

Summer

1. Radiant Slab (Cooling)
2. Vehicle Entry Doors (Closed)
3. Double Glazed Cavity (Exhaust Warm Air)
4. Ceiling Fans (Exhaust Air)
5. Louvered Skylights (Exhaust Air)

Winter

1. Radiant Slab (Heating)
2. Vehicle Entry Doors (Closed)
3. Double Glazed Cavity (Warm Air Circulation)
4. Ceiling Fans (Circulate Air)
5. Louvered Skylights (Closed)

d.

infrastructure

West 72nd Street Station

Location: **Manhattan, New York**
Client: **MTA New York City Transit**
Area: **40,275 sf**
Design/Completion: **1996/2003**
Awards: **New York Chapter Association of Builders and Contractors Award of Excellence**
Exhibition: **Subway Style: Architecture and Design in the New York City Subway Exhibit**
Joint Venture with Gruzen Samton LLP

The rehabilitation of one of Manhattan's busiest and most congested transit stations provides straphangers a much-improved subway travel experience. Located at West 72nd Street and Broadway, the site includes three landmarked elements — the existing station house, the track walls within the station, and the adjoining Verdi Park. The project included the renovation of the existing historic station house designed by Heins & LaFarge in the Flemish Renaissance style and built in 1904, the design of a new station house, and the creation of a new plaza linked to Verdi Park. The existing station house is on the National Register of Historic Places and is a New York City Landmark.

The new station house north of 72nd Street features new entrances and elevators, to better distribute the heavy passenger flow along the narrow platforms, relieve congestion, and provide ADA accessibility.

a.

b.

c.

a. Skylit entrance concourse
b. Comparative elevations
c. View looking north
d. Aerial views of new
   and historic station

d.

Columbus Circle Station

Location: **Manhattan, New York**
Client: **MTA New York City Transit**
Area: **250,000 sf**
Design/Completion: **2002/2009**
Joint Venture with Parsons Brinckerhoff

The Columbus Circle Station project organizes, rehabilitates, and restores this sprawling station complex at the intersection of the original Broadway Line and the more recent IND subway — underneath the newly renovated Columbus monument and fountain. Circular and oval elements at key entrances mark important station nodes, provide a sense of place, and facilitate way-finding for passengers. A retail galleria is planned for the subway passage between West 57th and West 58th Streets. Landmark elements of the IRT Station are preserved and restored. A major art installation by artist Sol LeWitt will grace the rehabilitated station. A new entrance at West 60th Street and Broadway makes entry to the complex more convenient and eases passenger flow, while new elevators provide handicapped accessibility to all platforms.

a.

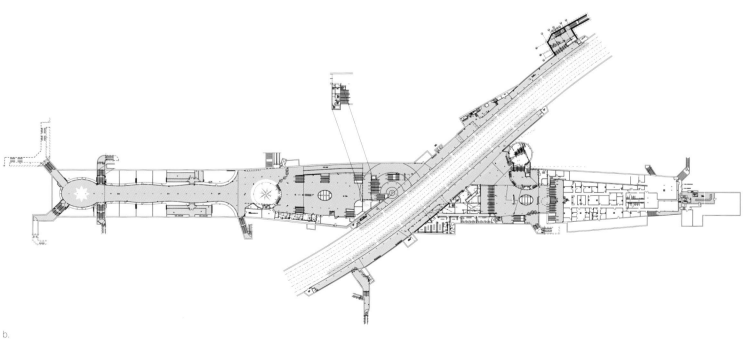

b.

a. View north at W. 57th St.
b. Mezzanine plan
c. Cutaway view
d. Sol LeWitt mural

c.

d.

Bowling Green Station Canopy

Location: **Manhattan, New York**
Client: **MTA New York City Transit**
Design/Completion: **2003/2007**

The entrance to the Bowling Green Station 4 & 5 Lines required protection from snow, rain, and wind for riders and escalators. Studies over many years had proposed covering this busy entrance located between the landmarked Customs House and historic Bowling Green Park — New York City's first park.

The new station canopy is a dramatic, transparent, curved steel and glass structure sensitive to its historic surroundings. Five stainless steel ribs project over the entrance, supporting a segmented glass roof and side wall panels. A granite base encloses the entrance stair and escalator and supports the canopy. The project involved close coordination with various public agencies and community organizations.

a.

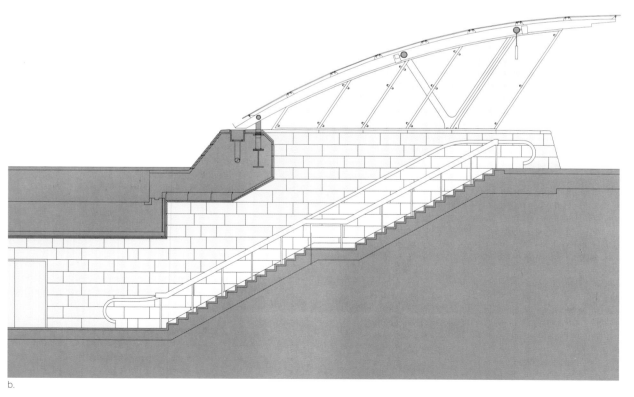

b.

a. Detail of structure
b. Section

Opposite page:
Entrance with
Customs House

No. 7 Subway Line Extension

Location: **Manhattan, New York**
Client: **MTA New York City Transit,**
New York City Department of City Planning,
Parsons Brinckerhoff
Design/Completion: **2002/2012**

The No. 7 Line subway extension from Times Square towards Jacob Javits Center is an integral part of the New York City Department of City Planning's redevelopment plan for the Far West Side of Manhattan. This major infrastructure upgrading will spur the development of new commercial and residential construction in a currently underdeveloped neighborhood. The project includes the design of two new subway stations — at 10th Avenue/41st Street and 11th Avenue/34th Street — new station entrances, several above-grade systems facilities buildings, and extensive coordination with the City's urban design master plan and proposed private development.

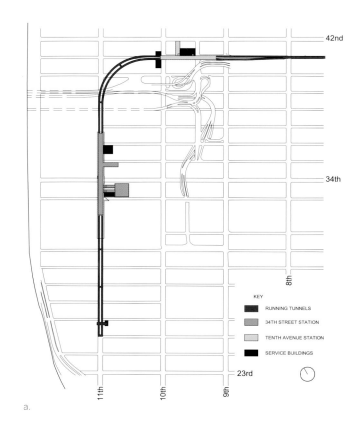

KEY

▮ RUNNING TUNNELS
▮ 34TH STREET STATION
▯ TENTH AVENUE STATION
▮ SERVICE BUILDINGS

a.

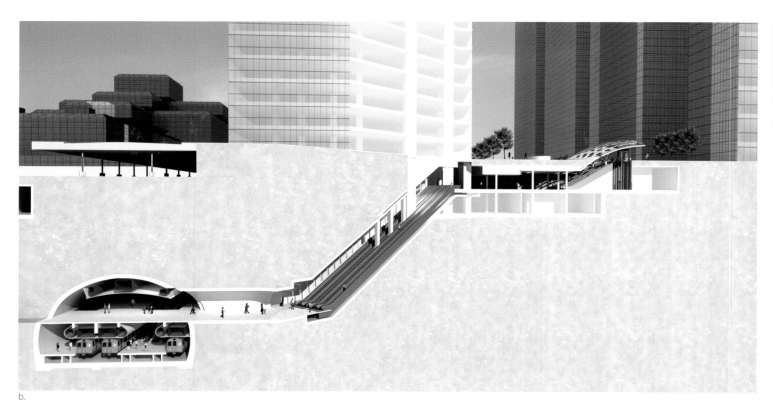

b.

c.

d.

a. Key plan
b. 34th St station
   section
c. 34th St station
   mezzanine level
d. 34th St station
   park entrance

a.

b.

c.

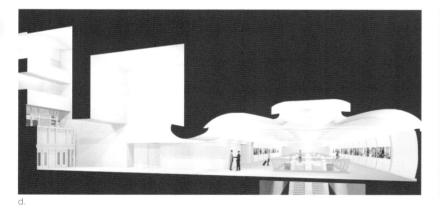

d.

e.

a. 10th Ave. station mezzanine
b. Park entrance at 34th St.
c. W. 41st St. station service building
d. Section at 10th Ave. station
e. Entrance at W. 42nd St.

Myrtle–Wyckoff Station

Location: **Brooklyn, New York**
Client: **MTA New York City Transit**
Area: **10,000 sf**
Design/Completion: **2000/2008**
Award: **Best Mass Transit Station Modernization, NY Construction Magazine**

The Myrtle–Wyckoff Station Complex is an important intermodal transit node on the Brooklyn/Queens border. The station complex consists of two stations on five levels. The Myrtle Avenue Station on the BMT "L" line is a center platform subway station two levels below grade, with a mezzanine one level below Wyckoff Avenue. The Wyckoff Avenue Station on the BMT "M" line is an elevated, split-island platform

station above Myrtle Avenue. The meeting of the two lines defines a triangular island bounded by Wyckoff, Myrtle, and Gates Avenues. The new Control Building entrance occupies a portion of this island, creating a dramatic entrance to both stations, and the connections between them. A glass-enclosed "lantern" housing a ceiling mosaic has become a neighborhood landmark. A consolidated employee facility and new

a.

street-level concession spaces are also included. Rehabilitation and infrastructure work bring the stations and control house to a state of good repair, and three new elevators make the stations ADA compliant. A pilot project for MTA's Design for the Environment, its sustainable features include daylighting and natural ventilation in the control house rotunda, lighting controls, and energy-saving mechanical systems.

b.

c.

a. View of entrance
b. Interior of lantern
c. Night view

Catskill–Delaware Ultraviolet Light Water Treatment Facility

Location: **Westchester County, New York**
Client: **Hazen & Sawyer/CDM**
Sponsor: **NYC Department of Environmental Protection**
Area: **100,000 sf**
Design/Completion: **2003/2009**

New York City possesses one of the greatest metropolitan water supply systems in the world. To enhance the safety of that system, the New York City Department of Environmental Protection is building an ultraviolet light disinfection facility in Westchester County, New York. Much of the processing facility is located below grade. Above-grade structures include administrative and personnel facilities, mechanical/electrical support facilities,

and a generator building. The structures are integrated with the topography of the site to reduce their visual impact and clad with pre-cast concrete panels to emphasize their visual organization. A series of walls extending into the landscape reinforces the relationship to the site. Planted roofs over portions of the subgrade structures, interior daylighting, and use of "green" materials and similar measures demonstrate a commitment to sustainable design.

a.

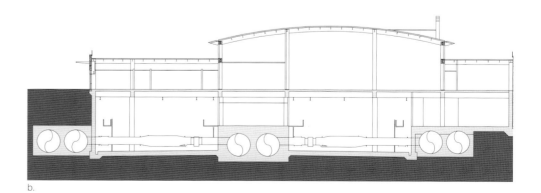

a. Entrance
b. Section of processing facility

b.

Brooklyn District 3 Garage

Location: **Brooklyn, New York**
Client: **NYC Department of Sanitation**
Area: **165,000 sf**
Design/Completion: **2004/2010**

This sanitation garage is located at the boundary between an industrial area and a growing residential neighborhood in Brooklyn. The structure will provide vehicle storage, washing, and repair facilities for the district fleet on the ground floor and covered employee parking on the second floor. Employee facilities and offices will be housed in a three-story zinc-clad "personnel block" facing Park Avenue. Circulation through the building is designed to facilitate the movement of large numbers of trucks, while minimizing the impact on local traffic patterns and adjacent residential buildings. A curved metal roof protects mechanical equipment and employee parking. Brick masonry façades with decorative banding provide human scale and respond to neighboring residential buildings. A green roof over a part of the structure will also enhance the neighborhood, while display cases for community sponsored exhibits are incorporated into the façade.

a.

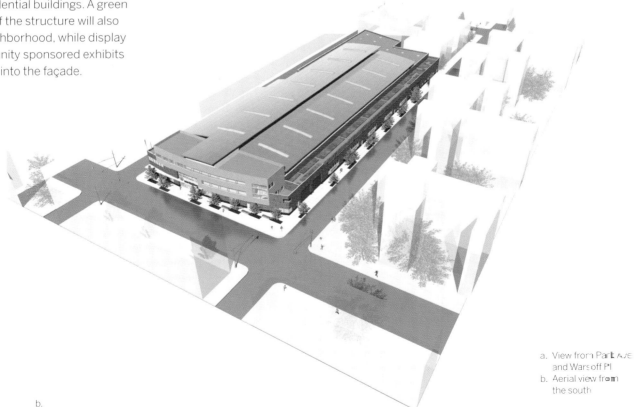

b.

a. View from Park Ave
and Wars off Pl
b. Aerial view from
the south

Manhattan Sanitation Districts 1/2/5 Garage

Location: **Manhattan, New York**
Client: **NYC Department of Sanitation**
Area: **425,000 sf**
Design/Completion: **2006/2013**
Awards: **Awarded through the New York City Design Excellence in Public Architecture Program**
In association with Weisz + Yoes

The NYC Department of Sanitation intends to construct a LEED Silver multistory, multidistrict garage at the corner of Spring Street and West Street in Lower Manhattan. The existing 85,000-square-foot site is a key gateway to the SoHo neighborhood overlooking the Hudson River/Hudson River Park. It is currently used by UPS as an open-air storage facility for semitrailers.

The new 425,000-square-foot building will provide separate personnel and truck storage facilities for three Community District Garages: Manhattan 1, Manhattan 2, and Manhattan 5. The building will be organized vertically with each district occupying its own floor (second, third, and fourth). A two-level personnel block at the south end of each garage floor will provide office, locker, and break room space for each district. A shared vehicle repair and wash facility will be located on the second floor with the Manhattan 1 Garage. A shared fueling facility will be located on the ground floor of the facility along with a separate semitrailer storage facility for UPS. A new salt storage facilty serving the Manhattan 1/2/5 garage will be constructed at the corner of Spring Street and Canal Street on the existing Manhattan 1 Garage site.

The design emphasizes a sense of openness and relationship to the community, as well as an environmentally responsible approach. The design addresses the sensitivity of the urban context, while meeting the complex functional and technical requirement for a multistory garage. The building is treated as having five "façades," including the exterior walls and roof, each designed in response to its exposure and surrounding context. Extensive use of movable fins and glazed elements lighten and reduce the apparent bulk of the building, provide a sense of openess, articulate the massing, provide scale, and integrate the building visually with the neighborhood. A green roof serves as a fifth façade to soften views, protect the roof membrane, and enhance storm water retention and thermal performance.

Other sustainable design strategies include: use of recycled and "green" materials, daylighting to reduce lighting loads, energy-efficient mechanical systems and building controls, and innovative ventilation approaches. The design team is also investigating other sustainable technologies such as photovoltaics and the use of rain harvesting as a source of water for vehicle washing.

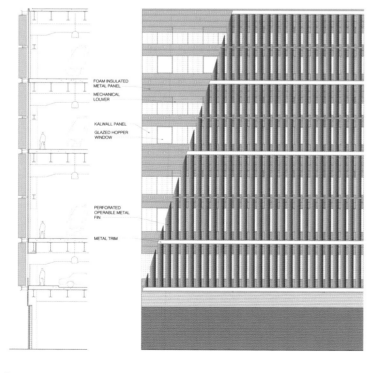

FOAM INSULATED METAL PANEL
MECHANICAL LOUVER
KALWALL PANEL
GLAZED HOPPER WINDOW
PERFORATED OPERABLE METAL FIN
METAL TRIM

a.

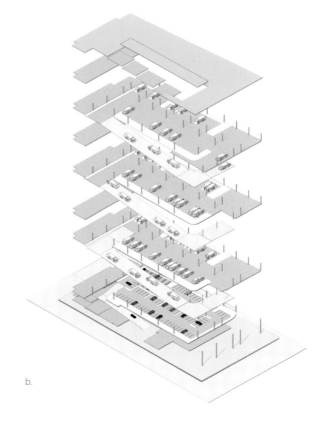

b.

c.

d.

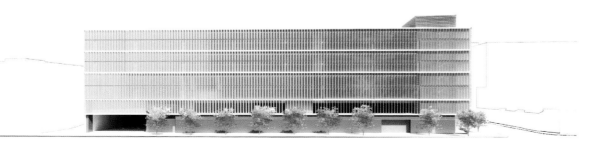

e.

a. Details of movable fins
b. Exploded view
c. View from West St.
d. West St. sidewalk
e. West elevation

Marine Transfer Stations

Location: **Manhattan, Brooklyn, Queens, New York**
Client: **Greeley & Hansen LLC, NYC Department of Sanitation**
Area: **80,000 sf each**
320,000 sf total
Design/Completion: **2003/2012**

As part of New York City's plan to make its solid waste disposal program more efficient and environmentally responsive, four new Marine Transfer Stations will place municipal waste into sealed containers for shipment by barge. These stations are based on a prototype design developed by our firm, with variations to respond to specific site conditions. The common design vocabulary unifies the designs of these stations and expresses their civic importance within the context of other marine structures on the New York City waterfront. Corrugated metal walls rise from pre-cast concrete bases. Translucent clerestories admit light during the day and glow at night. Standing-seam metal roofs and curving ventilation monitors cap the buildings. Gantry cranes, containers, and barges become kinetic design elements — demonstrating the transfer process occurring at these sites.

a.

1 E. 91st St.
2 North Shore
3 Hamilton Ave.
4 Southwest Brooklyn MTS

b.

c.

d.

a. Map of MTS sites
b. Southwest Brooklyn MTS
c. E. 91st St. MTS Manhattan
d. Aerial view

Dattner Architects Team

Partners

Paul Bauer AIA
Joseph Coppola AIA
Richard Dattner FAIA
Jeffrey S. Dugan AIA
Beth Greenberg AIA
Daniel Heuberger AIA, LEED AP
William Stein FAIA
R. John Woelfling AIA
Bernard Zipprich AIA LEED AP

Associates

Robin Auchincloss AIA, LEED AP
Joel Brown AIA
Michael Daniels AIA
Federico Del Priore AIA
Ruth Dresdner AIA
Steve Frankel AIA
David Grider AIA
Patricia Kettle AIA
Ira Mitchneck AIA
John Ziedonis AIA

Staff

Carlos Acevedo
FR Acuna
Venesa Alicea
Cristina Arbelaez
Ryi Aizu
Rosa Amaro
Ariad Beazer
Ryan Bergmann
Eran Birnbaum
Peter Branton
Nathan Burch
Arlene Calandria
Latika Chadha
Joon Cho
Jay Chokshi
Patrick Cheung LEED AP
Catherine Clark
David Cole
Julio Colon RA
Maria Clironomos
Paul Crespi
Cylvia Cruz-Beck
Guillermo B. Cubias
George Cumella Assoc. AIA
Jacky Curry RA
Stephen Dargo
Jean-Cedric DeFoy
Dalah Del Prado
Bob Drake

Stalin Duran
Rachel Ehrlich
Eric Epstein AIA, LEED AP
Maryam Fattaah
Fe Fruto
Kayo Fujiwara LEED AP
Masanori Fukuoka
Peter Gaito, Jr.
Iris Gartenbank
Daniel Ghosh LEED AP
Spilios Gianakopoulos
David Goldschmidt
Craig Graber
Jennifer Greene Assoc. AIA
Fatima Griffith
Perry Hall AIA
Huy Ho
Chan Hoang
Brian Hotchkiss AIA, LEED AP
Stella Hsu
Liz Huiza
Ijeoma D. Iheanacho
Jamil Isaac
Jonathan Jones
Kimberly Jones-Lenz
Aydan Kalkan AIA, LEED AP
Miyun Kang
Ben Karty AIA, LEED AP
John Kelly
Patricia Kettle RA
Cyrus Khodaparast
Somporn Khovitoonkij
Min Jung Kil LEED AP
Kwang Kim
Sunny Kim
Frederick M. Kincaid
Steve Knox
Adam Koffler
Sharon Kon
Emily Kotsaftis AIA, LEED AP
Matthew Kuria
Eugene Kwak
Boris Lakhman RA
John Lam AIA
Daniella LaRocca
David Levine AIA
Ming Lin
Sally Linan
Hanson Liu LEED AP
Stephen Lynch
Gia Maineiro LEED AP
Robert Markinson RA
Beata Matysiak
Terry McClenahan Assoc. AIA
Adam Meredith RA
Miguel Miranda
Ruth Mizrahi-Olti
Jessica Moore Lansdale AIA, LEED AP

Julio Morales
Karina Moya
Kristin Nelson RA
Brian Nesin AIA, LEED AP
Sarah Nordstrom
Datchie O'Dea
Toto Offemaria
Matt Ostrow
Gregory Overkamp
Stephen Paczkowski
Eric Perez
Marco Pirone
Robert Predmore
Katherine Prudente
Jeremy Reed
James Reynolds
Carole Richards
Patrick Rodgers
Sandra Rodriguez
Victor Rodriguez RA
Karla Roman
Sami Rubenfeld
Desire Rucker-Addison
Basima Rum Assoc. AIA
David Sachs
Deidre Salon
Cassandra Santiago
Jason Sargenti
Milan Savanovic
Robert Schwartz
Gabriel Seijas
Catherine Selby AIA, LEED AP
Ruta Shah
Adam Siegel LEED AP
Frances Soliven
Pete Sprung
Edward Stephens
Eve Strawhand
Eve Szentesi AIA
Matthew Thomas
Mary Tinitigan
Maurice Tobias
Bryan Tooze
Roxane Tsirigotis
Do-Yong Um
Almira Valdez
Ernesto Vela AIA
Patrick Ventker Intl. Assoc. AIA
James Vira RA
Daniel Walsh
Adam Watson AIA, LEED AP
Henry Weintraub
Wendy Wisbrun
Anita Wright
Jing Xiang
James Yi
John Young RA
Andre Zapata-Arboleda

Collaborators & Consultants

A. James deBruin & Sons
AB Consulting
Abel Bainnson Butz LLP
Accu Cost Construction Consultants, Inc.
Acentech Inc.
AG Consulting Engineering PC
AIA Engineers Ltd., PLLC Henry Hudson
AKRF
Ammann & Whitney
AMSEC M. Rosenblatt
Animation + Images
Ann Kale Associates, Inc.
Arup
Association for Energy Affordability
Atelier Ten
Atkinson Koven Feinberg Engineers LLP
Ballard King
Barbara Thayer Associates
Barker Mohandas, LLC
Barker Rinker Seacat Architecture
BB&L
Best Access Systems
BET Consultants
Betro Consulting Design
Beyer Blinder Belle Architects and Planners LLC
Blum Consulting Engineers, Inc.
Blumberg & Butter PC
Boom
Boswell Engineering Company
Bovis Lend Lease
Brandston Partnership
Bryan Cave
Burns Engineering, Inc.
Buro Happold
CBRE
CDM
Cerami & Associates, Inc.
Code Blue Design, LLC
Code Consultants Professional Engineers, PC
Construction Specifications, Inc.
Consulting Services Co.
Cosentini Associates
Costas Kondylis & Associates, PC
D'Onofrio General Contractors Corp.
Daniel Frankfurt PC
Datum
Design 2147 Ltd
DeSimone Consulting Engineers,
Development Consulting Services
DMJM Harris
Domingo Gonzalez Associates
Donna Walcavage Landscape Architecture
Doswell Productions
Ducibella Venter & Santore
DVL Consulting Engineers
Edelman Sultan Knox Wood Architects LLP
Ellana, Inc. – Construction Cost Consultants
Environmental Planning & Management, Inc.
Ettinger Engineering Associates
Feld, Kaminetzky & Cohen
Ferguson-Cox Associates
Flack+Kurtz Inc.
Fried, Frank, Harris, Shriver & Jacobson LLP
Future Tech Consultants
Gannett Fleming Engineers & Architects, PC
Genesys Engineering PC
George E. Berger & Associates LLC
George Langer Associates.
Glezen Fisher Associates

Global Green USA
Goldman Copeland Associates
Goldstein Associates
Greeley and Hansen
Grimshaw Architects
Gruskin Associates
Gruzen Samton LLP
GWK Architects
GVA Williams
GZA
Haley & Aldrich, Inc
Harvey, Marshall Berling Associates
Hayden McKay Lighting Design
Hazen and Sawyer, PC
Herbert L. Mandel Architect, PC
High Concrete Structures
Hill Associates/Hill, Devine & Gong
Hill International
Hirschen Singer & Epstein
I & L Consulting Inc.
Inigo Manglano-Ovalle
Ishmael Levya Architects PC
Israel Berger & Associates
JFK&M Consulting Group, Inc.
Jablonski Berkowitz Conservation Inc.
Janson Design Group
Jaros Baum & Bolles
JC Estimating
Jenkins & Huntington, Inc.
Joseph Biber
Judlau Contracting, Inc.
Kinetic Media, Inc.
Klein and Hoffman, Inc.
Kline Engineering PC
Kramer Levin Naftalis & Frankel
KS Engineers, PC
Kugler Associates
Lager Raabe
Lakhani & Jordan Engineers, PC
Landscape Architecture, LLC
Langan Engineering
Laszlo Bodak Engineer, PC
Lebowitz Gould Design, Inc.
Lee Weintraub Landscape Architecture
Leonard J. Strandberg Associates
Leslie E. Robertson Associates, RLLP
Lettire Construction
Levien & Co., Inc.
Levine Builders
Liam O'Hanlon Engineering, PC
Lilker Associates, PC
Li Saltzman Architects, PC
Logistics Consultant Inc.
Maitra Associates, PC
Mariano D. Molina, PC Consulting Engineers
Mathews Nielsen Landscape Architecture
McCaslin Associates, Inc.
McLaren Engineering Group
Metropolis Group
M-E Vogel Taylor Engineers, PC
MKW Associates Landscape Architects
Milber Makris Plousadis & Seiden LLP
Montrose Surveying Co., LLP
Milrose Consultants, Inc.
Munoz Engineering, PC
O'Dea Lynch Abbattista Consulting Engineers, LLP
Ocean and Coastal Consultants Inc.
Olympus International A.G.
Orda Management Corporation

Ostergaard Acoustical Associates
Paul Weiss Rifkind Wharton & Garrison LLP
PB World
Pentagram
Pelli Clarke Pelli Architects
Perini
Philip Habib & Associates
Plaza Construction Services
Post and Grossbard
Radii
Rampulla Associates Architects
Reginald D. Hough Architect
Renfro Design Group
Richard McElhiney Architect
RM Nelson Associates, Inc.
Robert Derector Associates
Robert Hickman
Robert Schwartz Associates
Robert Silman Associates, PC
Rodney D. Gibble Consulting Engineers
Romano-Gatland
Rosenwasser/Grossman Associates
SBLD Studio
Schmidt & Stacy
Schuman Lichtenstein Claman Efron
Sears Associates
Severud Associates Consulting Engineers PC
Shen Milsom & Wilke Inc.
Sherman Law
Simon Rodkin Consulting Engineers
Skanska/McKissack Partenership
Slater & Beckerman
SMWM Architects
Steven Winter Associates
Syska-Hennessey Group
The Berman Group
The Consortium For Worker Education
The Shaw Group
The Tyree Organization
Thinc Design
Thomas Balsley Associates
Thompson & Sears
Tillotson Design Associates
Tishman
TM Technology Partners
Todd Architectural Models
Toscano Clements Taylor
Turner Construction Company
URS Corporation
Van Deusen & Associates
Viridian Energy & Environmental, LLC
VJ Associates
Vollmer Associates LLP
Walter Associates Inc.
Water Technology Inc.
Weidlinger Associates
Weisz + Yoes Architecture
Wendy Feuer Public Art & Urban Design
Wesler-Cohen Associates
Wohl & O'Mara
Wojciechowski Design
Ysrael A. Seinuk PC
YU & Associates
Zetlin Strategic Communications

Clients

14th Street Merchants Association
92nd Street Y
Aramis
Amman & Whitney
Asphalt Green Inc.
Battery Park City Authority
Beginning With Children Inc.
Bellevue Association
Benerofe Properties
Berkeley Carroll School
Brooklyn College
Brooklyn Public Library
Cabrini Medical Center
Camp Dresser & McKee
Camp Rising Sun
CB Richard Ellis
City College of New York
City of Jerusalem
City of Tel Aviv
City University Law School
City University of New York
Clinique Laboratories
Columbia University
Columbia University School of Social Work
Columbia Cascade Timber Company
Community Development Agency of Newark
Community Development Agency of Yonkers
Congregation Rodeph Sholom
Consolidated Edison Company
Dallas Arboretum
Democratic National Convention Committee
District of Columbia
Dormitory Authority of the State of New York
Durst Organization
Dwight Englewood School
Empire State Development Corporation
Estée and Joseph Lauder Foundation
Estée Lauder Inc
Estée Lauder International
Federation Employment Guidance Services
Fresh Youth Initiatives
Goodwill Games 1998
Greeley & Hansen
Habitat for Humanity
Han Moory Church
Hardesty & Hanover Consulting Engineers
Harlem Congregations for
   Community Improvement
Hazen & Sawyer
Hertz Corporation
Hudson River Park Trust
Hunter College & Hunter College Campus School
Imobiliare, USA
Intrepid Museum / Intrepid Foundation
Jewish Board of Family and Children's Services
Jewish Community Center of Staten Island
Jewish Museum
Jonathan Rose Companies LLC
J.M. Kaplan Fund
KB Companies
Kingsbrook Jewish Medical Center
Kretchmer Development
Leake and Watts Family Services, Inc.
Manhattan Borough President
Merchandise Mart
Metropolitan Coordinating Council
   on Jewish Poverty
Metropolitan Development Agency of Tampa
Metropolitan Transportation Authority (MTA)

MTA Bridges & Tunnels
MTA Long Island Rail Road
MTA New York City Transit
MTA Metro North
MTA Triborough Bridge & Tunnel Authority
Model Cities, Highland Park, MI
Model Cities, Rochester, NY
Monadnock Corporation
Nassau County Parks & Recreation
National Children's Island Inc.
New York Athletic Club
New York City Administration for Children's
   Services
New York City Board of Education
New York Botanical Garden
New York City Department of City Planning
New York City Department of
   Design and Construction
New York City Department of
   Environmental Protection
New York City Department of
   Housing Preservation & Development
New York City Department of Sanitation
New York City Economic Development Corp.
New York City Educational Construction Fund
New York City Fire Department
New York City Housing Authority
New York City Parks and Recreation
New York City Police Department
New York City School Construction Authority
New York Foundation for Senior Citizens
New York Presbyterian Hospital
New York Public Library
New York State Division of
   Housing and Community Renewal
New York State Office of General Services
New York State Office of Mental Health
New York State Office of
   Parks, Recreation & Historic Preservation
New York State Urban Development Corporation
New York University
New York University Medical Center
New Visions New York
Norden Systems
NYC 2012 Olympic Committee
NYNEX
Origins, Inc.
Parsons Brinkenhoff
Parsons Transportation
PB Americas
Pfizer Corporation
Phipps Houses Group
Port Authority of New York & New Jersey
Prescriptives, Inc.
Princeton University
Queens Borough President
Queens College
Queens Public Library
Queens West Development Corporation
Red Apple Group
Red Hook Planning
Republic National Bank
Roag Inc. & Two Chestnuts Inc.
Robin Hood Foundation
Rockrose Development Corp.
Rosenthal Jewish Community Center
Rutgers University
San Francisco Museum of Modern Art
Schomburg Center for Research in Black Culture

Services for the Underserved
Settlement Housing Fund
Sheltering Arms Children's Services
Soros Fund Management
State University Construction Fund
State University of New York at Stony Brook
Steiner Equities Group, LLC
Stone & Webster
Streetscape Inc.
Street Squash
Takapausha Museum
Temple Beth El Chappaqua
The Salvation Army
Time Warner Cable Inc.
Town of Cortlandt
Town of Secaucus
Triglia Development
Union Free School District 13
United States Army Corps of Engineers
United States Department of
   Housing and Urban Development
University of Pennsylvania
United States General Services Administrator
United States Postal Service
Vornado Realty Trust
Washington Heights & Inwood
   Development Corp.
Wave Hill
Webb and Brooker
Westchester Association for Retarded Citizens
Westchester Children's Museum
Weston United Community Renewal, Inc
Whitman Laboratories, UK
Whitney Museum of American Art
Yale Club of New York
YMCA of Greater New York
Yonkers Public Schools
Zucker Organization

Selected Publications

205 East 59th Street

"Buyers Have Designs on New East Side
Tower." *Real Estate Weekly* (May 2004)
"In New Buildings, Buying Into Cool."
The New York Times (Nov 28, 2004)
"Urban Pleasures in the Most
Unlikely Places."
The New York Sun (Jul 25, 2005)

72nd St. Subway Station

"A West Side Developer's Other Side."
The New York Times (Aug 28, 2005)
"Shiny and New at 72nd Street:
Sunny Subway Entrance Draws Raves."
The New York Sun (Oct 30, 2002)

Bowling Green Subway Entrance

"Made for Manhattan: One day, one city,
countless amounts of glass."
Glass Magazine (Jan 2008)
"New Entrance a Jewel in an Historic Setting."
www.lowermanhattan.info (Mar 3, 2007)
"Touching Up Bowling Green."
The New York Sun (Jun 26, 2007)

Bronx Library Center

"A Bronx Tale." *Building Design & Construction
Magazine* (May 2006)
"A Role Model for Energy Use and Environmental
Sustainability."
Profile Architecture magazine 05 (2007)
"An Open Book."
Contract Magazine (Apr 2006)
"Branching Out."
Architectural Record magazine (May 2006)
"Bronx Library Center."
Glass Magazine (May 2006)
"Checking it Out."
Eco-structure (Sep 2006)
"Clear Reflection of its World."
Newsday (Jan 19, 2006)
"Dattner Architects –
Richard Dattner and Bill Stein."
Competitions (Summer 2007)
"Ingram 'un mundo ideal en El Bronx."
Hoy Nueva York (Jan 18, 2006)
Keeping it Green – The Bronx Library Center
The New York Public Library Press (2006)
"Let the Sun Shine In."
GreenSource (Jan 2007)
"Libraries = Cultural Icons."
American Library Journal (Apr 2006)
"New Bronx Branch to Be System's
First Green Facility."
New York Construction (Jul 2005)
"New Bronx Library Meets Old Need."
The New York Times (Jan 16, 2006)
"New Central Library to open in the Bronx."
Crain's NewYorkBusiness.com (Jan 6, 2006)

"New Library Checks In."
New York Daily News (Jan 18, 2006)
"One Library Out of Many."
The New York Sun (Jul 26, 2007)
"Pumping Up The Volumes."
Time Out New York (Jan 19–25, 2006)
"The Approval Matrix."
New York Magazine (Jan 23, 2006)
"The Bronx Does Design."
Oculus (Spring 2006)
"The Greenest Branch."
New York Spaces (Mar 2008)
"Top 10 LEED Projects."
Interiors & Sources (Oct 2006)

Cat/Del UV Water Treatment

"Drinking Water: New York City Moves
Forward on UV Facility."
Civil Engineering (Oct 2003)

Consolidated Edison of New York

"A Building In Tune With The Traffic."
The New York Times (Apr 14, 2002)
"Nourishing the Power Plant."
New Yorker by Nature (Feb 13, 2006)

Coney Island Commons

"Swim, Compute, Confab at the
New Coney Center."
The Daily News (Jan 11, 2007)
"Coney Island's Renaissance:
New Mixed Use Development is First Step
Toward Reviving Area."
The Architect's Newspaper
(Feb 1, 2007)
"The Next New York."
The Architect's Newspaper (Aug 1, 2007)

David and Joyce Dinkins Gardens

"A Green Future for Affordable Housing."
Lessons Learned magazine (Aug 17, 2006)
"Affordable Green Housing in New York."
www.treehugger.com (Apr 1, 2008)
"An Integrated Approach to Green Design."
Institute for Urban Design magazine
(May 2007)
"Can Affordable Housing be Sustainable?"
AIArchitect (Feb 1, 2008)
"David & Joyce Dinkins Gardens: First Green
Exclusively Affordable Housing Development in
Harlem."
www.greenbuildingsnyc.com (Apr 1, 2008)
"Development That Is Mindful of the Planet and
the Budget."
The New York Times (Apr 3, 2008)
"Going green, affordably – designing sustainable
housing on a nonprofit budget."
Residential Architect (Mar 2008)

"Harlem eco-building is first for low-income."
am New York (Apr 1, 2008)
"Man with a Mission: Jonathan Rose makes the
world greener while building affordable housing."
Entrepreneur magazine (Dec 2007)
"New Horizon, Evolution of Affordable Housing
Sector May Spur More Development."
New York Construction (Aug 2007)
"Sustainable Affordable Housing is No Myth."
eOculus (Feb 5, 2008)
"The Next New York."
The Architect's Newspaper (Aug 1, 2007)

Dwight Englewood School Klein Campus Center

"A new building gives focus to a private school's
campus."
Archrecord.construction.com (Jul 2007)
"Best of 2006: Dwight Englewood School Klein
Campus Center Project"
New York Construction (Dec 2006)
"Pride in Architecture."
The New York Times (Oct 28, 2007)

Hudson River Park Segments 6 and 7

"An Urban Work in Progress – Clinton Cove
Park."
Recreation Management (Jul/Aug 2006)
"Civic Lessons at the Water's Edge:
Dattner Architects."
Oculus (Summer 2004)
"Clinton Cove Park Opens."
The Architect's Newspaper (Jun 22, 2005)
"How the West Was Done."
Landscape Architecture (Aug 2004)
"Hudson River Park's Clinton Cove Park."
Real Estate & Construction Review
New York Tri-State Edition (Volume 4, 2006)
"Hudson River Park – Clinton Cove Park and Pier
96 Boathouse."
New York Construction (Dec 2005)
"Hudson River Park Pier 96 Boathouse."
Sports and Recreational Facilities (2005)
"New West Side Story."
Landscape Architecture (Aug 2007)
"The River's Edge."
Interior Design (Sep 2005)

Intrepid, Sea, Air and Space Museum
Master Plan and Renovations

"Anchors Aweigh."
Newsday (Sep 5, 2006)
"Dattner Architects – Richard Dattner
and Bill Stein."
Competitions (Summer 2007)
"Intrepid Museum to Set Sail for $55M Facelift."
Newsday (Jul 4, 2006)
"Intrepid Will Cross River for Refitting, Then
Return to a Rebuilt Pier."
The New York Times (Jul 4, 2006)
"Veterans Day parade to salute
USS Intrepid in 2008."
Newsday (Jul 27, 2007)

IS/HS 362 Bronx

"New York, New Schools."
The Architect's Newspaper (Sep 22, 2006)

Jewish Community Center of Staten Island

"Growing Pains On Staten Island." *Jewish Week*
(Jan 21, 2000),
"New JCC Building is Dedicated in Sea View."
Staten Island Advance (Oct 27, 2007)
"Top Honors for 3 Commercial Structures."
Staten Island Advance (Dec 7, 2007)

McBurney YMCA

"McBurney YMCA."
Real Estate and Construction Review
(Volume 4, 2005)

Myrtle Avenue Development

"Brooklyn Reaches for the Skies."
New York Post (Nov 1, 2007)
"Massive Retail Space Being Assembled on
Brooklyn's Myrtle Avenue."
Brooklyn Daily Eagle (Jan 4, 2008)
"The Next New York."
The Architect's Newspaper (Aug 1, 2007)

NYC Administration for Children's Services Intake Center and Satterwaite Training Facility

"Designed to Be Almost as Welcoming
as a Mother's Arms."
The New York Times (Sep 06, 2001)
"New Center for Foster Children Echoes
Changes in an Agency."
The New York Times (Jun 01, 2001)
"NYC Boosts Gren Buildings: Guide Offers
Design Expertise to Owners and Operators."
Energy User News (Sep 1999)

Pier 40 – The People's Pier

"People's Pier vs. Performing Arts Center
Pitched for Pier 40."
The Villager (Dec/Jan 2006–2007)
"Pier Pressure Builds as Decision Day Nears."
Downtown Express (Jan 24–31, 2008)
"Village Wants to Keep Its Fields as They Are."
The New York Times (Jan 30, 2008)

Primary School 276 in Battery Park City

"A New 'Green' School for Lower Manhattan."
The New York Times (Nov 13, 2007)
"City to Build Green School in Lower Manhattan."
Crain's New York Business (Nov 13, 2007)

"Designers Give BPC School Preview."
Tribeca Trib (Dec 1, 2007)
"Governor Spitzer, Mayor Bloomberg and
Speaker Silver Announce Plans to Build City's
First-Ever Green School in Battery Park City."
www.nyc.gov (Nov 13, 2007)
"'Green'-lighted Eco-friendly School."
New York Post (Nov 14, 2007)
"Green School Design."
Downtown Express (Mar 7–13, 2008)
"NYC Unveils Plan to Build City's
First Green School."
Building Design + Construction magazine
(Nov 20, 2007)

Ray and Joan Kroc Center

"Community Center or Center
of the Community?"
Good News! (Mar 2007)

Schomburg Center for Research in Black Culture

"Celebrating the Grand Opening
of the New Schomburg."
Africana Heritage (Volume 7, 2007)
"Harlem's Cultural Anchor in a Sea of Ideas."
The New York Times (May 11, 2007)
"Harlem in Residence: Community,
Relationships and Creativity."
The Studio Museum in Harlem Magazine
(Summer 2007)
"Schomburg Center for Research
in Black Culture."
Glass Magazine (Apr 2007)
"Schomburg Center for Research in Black
Culture unveils $22 million renovation."
Amsterdam News (May 17, 2007)

Steiner Studios

"Dream Factory: The Brooklyn Navy Yard
goes Hollywood."
Oculus (Winter, 2004/2005)
"More Studio Space as Entertainment
Production Increases in NYC."
MetroFilm (Winter Edition 2007)
"On the Set at Navy Yard,
It's Hollywood vs. a Blue-Collar Past."
The New York Times (Dec 13, 2003)
"On Brooklyn Back Lot, Finally, Some Action."
The New York Times (Jul 21, 2003)
"Steiner Studios To Debut With Mel Brooks'
'Producers' Remake."
The Brooklyn Eagle (Oct 01, 2004)
"The Golden Age of Brooklyn."
Metro (Jan 31, 2006)

State University of New York at Stony Brook Athletic Stadium

"Best Stadium: Kenneth P. Lavalle Stadium State
University of New York at Stony Brook, N.Y."
Ascent (Oct 2006)
"SUNY Stony Brook Takes to the Field."
Ascent (Fall 2006)

University of Pennsylvania Pottruck Health & Fitness Center

"Getting Fit." *Buildings* (Oct, 2003)
"University of Pennsylvania Pottruck
Health & Fitness Center."
Sports and Recreational Facilities (2005)

Via Verde – The Green Way

"Architectural Firm Active in Brooklyn Part of
Winning Team to Build Sustainable Housing."
Brooklyn Daily Eagle (Mar 22, 2007)
"Beauty and the Bronx: An innovative mixed
income housing project will bring sustainabl
living to hip hop's home."
Vive Magazine (Mar 2008)
"Best New Affordable Housing – Via Verde."
New York Magazine (Dec 17, 2007)
"Cleaning up New York's Buildings."
Gotham Gazette (Oct 15, 2007)
"Come Together: Integrating Design."
Harvard Design Magazine
(Fall 2007/Winter 2008)
"Dattner Architects – Richard Dattner
and Bill Stein."
Competitions (Summer 2007)
"Man with a mission: Jonathan Rose makes the
world greener while building affordable housing."
Entrepreneur magazine (Dec 2007)
"New Horizon, Evolution of Affordable Housing
Sector May Spur More Development."
New York Construction (Aug 2007)
"New Housing New York Legacy Project:
Lessons Learned."
Oculus (Fall 07)
"New Housing New York Winner Imagines a
Sustainable South Bronx."
Architectural Record (Jan 2007)
"N.Y. Selects Designers/Developers for First
'Green' Public Housing Contest."
Multi-Housing News (Jan 2007)
"Sustainable Affordable Housing is No Myth."
eOculus (Feb 5, 2008)
"Team's Green Vision Wins Competition for
Affordable Housing."
Real Estate Weekly (Jan 2007)
"The Green Way: Via Verde, Bronx, NY."
Institute for Urban Design magazine (May 2007)

Westchester Children's Museum

"Plan for Children's Museum
at Historic Site Faces Delay."
The New York Times (Jan 27, 2008)

Selected Awards & Exhibitions

2008

New York City Green Building Award
US Environmental Protection Agency
Battery Park City Parks Conservancy
Maintenance Facility

Citation for Design Excellence
New York State American Institute of Architects
Bronx Library Center

Silver Award of Distinction
Brick Industry Association
Myrtle Wyckoff Station Complex

Neighborhood Achievement Award
City of New York and Small Business Services
David & Joyce Dinkins Gardens

Multi-Housing's Top Architects
Multi-Housing News magazine
Dattner Architects

Best Mass Transit Project
New York Construction magazine
Myrtle Wyckoff Subway Station Modernization

Award of Merit
New York Construction magazine
Pelham Parkway Subway Station Modernization

Award of Merit
New York Construction magazine
Pier 86 Renovation

Building America Award
New York Real Estate and Construction Review
Schomburg Center for Research in Black Culture

Building America Award
New York Real Estate and Construction Review
Laura Rothenberg Bronchoscopy-Endoscopy
Suite at New York Presbyterian Hospital

Building America Award
New York Real Estate and Construction Review
Myrtle Wyckoff Subway Station Modernization

Building America Award
New York Real Estate and Construction Review
David & Joyce Dinkins Gardens

2007

Award of Excellence
Sustainable Buildings Industry Council
Bronx Library Center

Culture Awards Best New Affordable Housing
New York Magazine
Via Verde – The Green Way

Merit Award for Excellence in Architecture
New Jersey American Institute of Architects
Dwight Englewood School Klein Campus Center

Berlin – New York Dialogues: Building in Context
Exhibit, Center for Architecture
Via Verde – The Green Way

Merit Award
New York Construction magazine
Laura Rothenberg Bronchoscopy-Endoscopy
Suite at New York Presbyterian Hospital

New New York: Fast Forward Exhibit
Architectural League of New York
Ten New York City Projects

The Green House
National Building Museum
Via Verde – The Green Way

Powerhouse New Housing New York
Center for Architecture
Via Verde – The Green Way

2006

Architecture Firm Award
New York State American Institute of Architects
Dattner Architects

Edison Lighting Award of Excellence
General Electric Lighting
Bronx Library Center

Edison Lighting Excellence in Sustainable Design
General Electric Lighting
Bronx Library Center

Award of Merit
International Interior Design Association /
Illuminating Engineering Society
Bronx Library Center

Award of Merit
New York State American Institute of Architects
Clinton Cove Pier 96 Boathouse

New Building Award
Queens & Bronx Building Association
Jewish Community Center of Staten Island

Best Monographic Museum Show
U.S. Art Critics Association
Eva Hesse Exhibition at Jewish Museum

Merit Award
New York Construction magazine
Dwight Englewood School Klein Campus Center

New York City Green Building Award
US Environmental Protection Agency
Bronx Library Center

Institutional Finalist
Environmental Design Construction magazine
Bronx Library Center

Award of Excellence
Precast Concrete Industry
SUNY Stony Brook Stadium

Waterfront Conference Selected Project
National Museum of the American Indian
Clinton Cove Pier 96 Boathouse

Community Facility Category Award
Brooklyn Chamber of Commerce
Building Brooklyn Awards Dodge YMCA

Building Team Silver Award
Building Design Construction magazine
Bronx Library Center

Plaque of Honor
New York Real Estate and Construction Review
West 72nd Street Subway Rehabilitation

Plaque of Honor
New York Real Estate and Construction Review
McBurney YMCA

2005

Best of New Construction Award
New York Construction magazine
Clinton Cove Boathouse

Award of Merit
Concrete Industry Board SUNY Stony Brook
Athletic Stadium

Industrial Category Award
Brooklyn Chamber of Commerce
Steiner Studios

2004

Award of Recognition
Concrete Industry Board
205 East 59th Street Building

The American Dream Post 9/11 Exhibit
Salmagundi Club
The New World Trade Center;
Keys of Remembrance Memorial

Award of Excellence
New York Chapter Association of
Builders and Contractors
West 72nd Street Subway Station Rehabilitation

Subway Style: Architecture and Design in the
New York City Subway
Exhibit Grand Central Station Gallery;
Paine Weber Gallery
West 72nd Street Subway Station Rehabilitation
and Myrtle Wyckoff Station Rehabilitation

2003

New Construction Awards
Buildings magazine
University of Pennsylvania David Pottruck
Health and Fitness Center

Best Monographic Museum Show
U.S. Art Critics Association
Eva Hesse Exhibition at SFMOMA

2002

Award of Recognition
Concrete Industry Board
Coney Island Comfort & Lifeguard Stations

Excellence in Historic Preservation Award
Preservation League of New York State
ACS New Children's Center

Excellence in Design Award
Art Commission of the City of New York
Brooklyn District 1 & 4 Garages & Administration
Building

2001

Honorable Mention
Queens County Builders and
Contractors Association, Inc.
PS 228 Early Childhood Center

Preservation Award
New York Landmarks Conservancy;
NYC Department of Design and Construction
ACS New Children's Center

Public Art Exhibition
NYC Department of Design and Construction
ACS Children's Center; Engine Company 75

1994

Thomas Jefferson Award for Public Architecture
American Institute of Architects

1992

Medal of Honor
American Institute of Architects New York
Chapter

Photo Credits

Jeff Goldberg/ESTO
(pp. 6–7, 10, 12–21)
SHÜCO
(p. 10)
Ruggero Vanni, Vanni Archives
(pp. 6–7, 22–25, 30, 34–39, 42–45, 51, 63, 72
74–75, 76–77, 80–81, 83–89, 90–91 93, 106–107,
123, 128-129)
Richard Dattner
(pp. 6–7, 26, 28–29, 46–47, 50, 75, 82, 84–85, 133)
John Bartelstone
(pp. 32, 40)
Laurie Zucker
(pp. 53–55)
Wade Zimmerman
(pp. 6, 52)
Bruce Katz
(pp. 78–79, 80–81)
Kevin Chu + Jessica Paul
(pp. 6–7, 94–95, 102–103)
Cervin Robinson
(pp. 116, 118–119)
Norman McGrath
(pp. 6–7)
Laura Rosen
(pp. 6–7)
Pete Sprung
(pp. 6–7, 102–103)
Scott Frances/ESTO
(pp. 6–7)
Peter Mauss/ESTO
(pp. 6–7)

Rendering & Graphics Credits

Dattner Architects
(pp. 6–7, 26–27, 31–33, 48–49, 66–67, 68–69, 76,
82–83, 92–93, 96–97, 100–101, 104–105, 109
110–113, 115, 130–133)
Pelli Clarke Pelli
(pp. 6, 114)
3d Win
(pp. 32–33, 41, 86–87 133)
Dattner + Grimshaw Architects
(pp. 56–61)
PB Americas
(pp. 124–125)
Animation & Images
(pp. 70–71, 125, 127, 134–135)
Azalia Linan Bianchini
(pp. 64–65, 105, 120, 125–126)
Matt Ostrow
(pp. 109, 125, 127)
Abigail Kirsch
(p. 106)
Lee Weintraub
(p. 57)

Published in Australia in 2009 by
The Images Publishing Group Pty Ltd
ABN 89 059 734 431
6 Bastow Place, Mulgrave, Victoria 3170, Australia
Tel: +61 3 9561 5544 Fax: +61 3 9561 4860
books@imagespublishing.com
www.imagespublishing.com

Copyright © The Images Publishing Group Pty Ltd 2009
The Images Publishing Group Reference Number: 794

All rights reserved. Apart from any fair dealing for the purposes
of private study, research, criticism or review as permitted under
the Copyright Act, no part of this publication may be reproduced,
stored in a retrieval system or transmitted in any form by any means,
electronic, mechanical, photocopying, recording or otherwise,
without the written permission of the publisher.

National Library of Australia Cataloguing-in-Publication entry:
Title: Dattner Architects.
ISBN: 978 1 86470 285 9 (hbk.)
Subjects: Richard Dattner & Partners, Architects.
                Architecture, American—New York (N.Y.)
                Public architecture—New York (N.Y.)
                Architectural firms—New York (N.Y.)
Dewey Number: 720.97471

Layout and design by Marco Raab and Sidney Blank
SuperMetric, New York City
www.supermetric.com

Coordinating editor: Beth Browne

Production by The Graphic Image Studio Pty Ltd, Mulgrave, Australia
www.tgis.com.au

Digital production by Chroma Graphics (Overseas) Pte Ltd, Singapore

Printed on 150gsm HannoArt Silk Matt by Everbest Printing Co. Ltd.,
in Hong Kong/China

IMAGES has included on its website a page for special
notices in relation to this and its other publications.
Please visit www.imagespublishing.com.

Every effort has been made to trace the original source of copyright
material contained in this book. The publishers would be pleased to
hear from copyright holders to rectify any errors or omissions.

The information and illustrations in this publication have been
prepared and supplied by Dattner Architects. While all reasonable
efforts have been made to source the required information and
ensure accuracy, the publishers do not, under any circumstances,
accept responsibility for errors, omissions and representations
express or implied.